12-20-74

Driving Out the Devils

Sybil Leek

Driving Out the Devils

FOUNDED 1838

GPPS

G. P. Putnam's Sons
New York

Foreword

All authors feel a sense of relief when a book is finished. Mailing a manuscript brings an intense feeling of satisfaction and sometimes a little apprehension, the author wondering if an editor will like it. With luck, this feeling does not last because there is generally another contract to be fulfilled. I have always felt a wonderful sense of relief on finishing a book, but I have never felt anything like the emotions experienced on completing this particular one.

The unusual circumstances under which it was written contributed to this. Shortly after signing the contract, I was taken ill with a mysterious sickness. This in itself was a shock because for years I have managed to evade going to see any doctor and have been delighted to enjoy very good health. One night my son Julian arrived at my condominium and found me literally choking to death. He miraculously found a doctor who was prepared to make a house call late in the evening. I recovered very quickly and within two days fulfilled my plans to go to London to do some extra research in the British Museum. Considering the fact that I had been at death's door through choking and running a ferociously high temperature, it was a miracle to be able to travel.

Three weeks later I was back in Florida ready to start on the new book.

For many years I have had a regular routine for writing. I enjoy writing early in the morning until eleven A.M. Then I take a break in the afternoon to go on the beach, sail or simply do nothing. At nine P.M. I start to write again and continue until about three A.M. every day.

I have been called a disciplined writer because of this routine, and it has proved very productive. Early in May, 1974, I began this book, starting at nine P.M. I have an ideal place to write, high up over the Atlantic Ocean in a penthouse. When the last of my sons got married I decided to modernize my way of life. My companions at that time were four elderly, much traveled Siamsese cats and two small parrots. The cats love to sit around me while I type, and on one particular night there was nothing unusual happening to begin with. The first few pages flowed freely and then I began to feel terribly cold. As I got up to check the windows, a great gust of wind sent everything flying from the desk. At first I thought I had left several windows open and was experiencing a crosscurrent of wind. But the windows were closed and the air conditioning was set at seventy-two degrees. I continued to work but with some uneasiness; I felt a strange presence in the apartment. The cats fixed their crossed blue eyes on a distant spot, hackles up and tails fanned out as they always are when the cats are angry or disturbed. With one mind they made a rapid exit to my bedroom and stayed there for the rest of the night. For the next few weeks writing became more and more difficult. Pictures fell from the walls; the two chandeliers lurched crazily against the ceiling; the same coldness crept into the house.

6

Some nights were much worse than others. Papers were thrown around; several letters from the typewriter exploded in my face; and in three weeks I got through three old and trusty typewriters.

The cats preferred to stay in my large bedroom, although I always left the door open. Doors in the house opened and closed while I sat at the typewriter. I maintained the air conditioning, but the long drapes near me would frequently billow up and remain suspended in the air for several moments.

My two birds are normally very talkative, and the only way to keep them silent is to cover them. One night they began to create a disturbance, fluttering pitifully up and down in the cage. I found one dead when I lifted the cover. Since that day the surviving bird has never said one word. Nauseating odors sometimes filled the air as books fell from shelves. A large neon light in the office exploded, scattering fine fragments of glass all over the desk. It seemed time to exorcise the apartment—which I did three times during the writing of this book.

I cannot say I was afraid, but I was very angry. I have probably visited more haunted houses than anyone else in the world, and I resented the intrusion into my own household of whatever it was. Normally I sleep very well and thrive on four hours each night; if I go to bed at three A.M. I can get up at seven A.M. feeling very fresh and anxious to get on with some work. I went for two weeks with very little sleep and always invaded by horrible nightmares. Tiredness crept up on me.

Every morning papers had to be tidied up and many found their way into strange places. For instance, I am not accustomed to filing any papers in saucepans or the big pot I reserve for making marmalade. But I found letters to my editor hidden away in such places! Nearly every night the lights would flicker, go very low and then blaze into brightness, and the same old thudding noises, growling sounds and destruction went on.

I was well aware that after an exorcism, phenomena are apt to become more intense. My household exorcisms were no exception. One night my heavy, very comfortable typing chair was snatched away from me and I slipped to the ground. On several nights when I went to take a bath, my legs, arms, back of the neck and lower part of my back were covered with ugly bruises. As I write this I have a horrible red blistered bruise on my ankle. It has not responded to treatment as it should have done.

A few days before the manuscript was finished, I felt utterly tired and psychically weary as well. My daughter-in-law went to the dishwasher to remove the clean dishes from the machine. A heavy butcher knife flew up from the machine, hitting her in the face. My son went to her aid and, as he reached the kitchen, a large bottle of wine hurled itself through the air from the top of the refrigerator, striking him on the side of his chest before crashing to pieces on the floor. Neither was seriously injured. There were slight nicks where the knife had hit my daughter-in-law's face; as it moved from the machine, the knife had turned so that the blunt side hit her rather than the cutting edge. The cats and bird remained scared for weeks, although they are rarely disturbed by anything. After all, they have traveled the length and breadth of the United States with me and are used to such strange noises as planes taking off and landing.

Finally the manuscript was finished. The icy winds ceased, also the growling noises and the nauseating smells. Wearily I packed up the mass of papers and took the manuscript to the mail. The mouse was peaceful that night, but I did not sleep. I emerged into the world to meet with friends again only to be told by them that I looked "awful." Some of them said very kindly, "We knew you must be ill because we haven't seen you for some time. You must be careful, have a nice long convalescence." They meant well, and I could not tell them that all I had done was to write another book. I canceled several lectures—something I have never done before in my life—and concentrated on purifying the house by ritual. Whatever evil entity accompanied me in the writing of this book seems to have gone. My sense of humor returned and I toyed with the idea of asking my publishers for insurance money. Instead I settled for heaving the biggest sigh of relief when the manuscript left the house. Peace reigns again, and may it continue to do so. The devil, demons, poltergeists and things-that-go-bump-in-the-night have no place in this apartment. I value my privacy and peace of mind.

SYBIL LEEK

Contents

Foreword   5

CHAPTER

1   Turbulence in Texas   17

2   Nightmare in Galveston   33

3   Evolution of the Devil   50

4   Demonology   62

5   Possession in the Bible   76

6   Hostages of the Damned   89

7   With Authority and Power
He Commandeth!   101

8   Exorcism—the Waterloo of Devils   119

9   Shields Against the Devil   136

10   Attitudes of the Churches
Toward Exorcism   147

11   Mass Possession   164

12   All This, and Hell, Too!   183

13   The Devil's Adversaries   205

14   The Psyche—the Achilles'
Heel of Man   222

I am most grateful for the courtesy and help given to me by Mrs. Sanders of the Cape Canaveral Public Library and members of the staff of the British Museum.
Also to my family for their patience with me at the time of writing this book.

Driving Out the Devils

Chapter One

Turbulence in Texas

On December 15, 1969, we decided to move from our home in Florida to Houston, Texas. I was enchanted by the thought and my persuasive tongue easily sold the idea to my two sons, Stephen and Julian, who had recently emigrated from England. I had visited Houston many times, loved the city as well as the state, and had made many friends there. I felt it was time to move on from Florida, although I did not give up my house in Melbourne Beach.

Most of all, I was intrigued with the house I had bought in Houston—a strange little place that looked as if it should be in Germany, by a quiet road near the university. I fell in love with the house because it resembled a miniature castle, complete with a large turret over the front door. Not one room was symmetrical, and the bedrooms were cut off from the living quarters of the house by a circular corridor. The heavy wooden doors and the polished hardwood floors pleased me most of all because they reminded me of England. (I could see my antique Persian carpets showing off to great advantage in this house.) And to

17

complete the picture of a most desirable residence, there was a wonderful garden and a carriage house converted to an apartment over the garage.

It seemed as if a wonderful new life were about to open up, with all the challenges that make anything new a meaningful experience. Although I had once lived in New York, I have never thought of myself as a city dweller and had always rejected the idea until I saw Houston. After many years in the quiet backwaters of Florida I felt culturally deprived and longed for such things as symphony concerts, theaters, supper clubs, and interesting people to talk with. Florida appealed to me mainly for its waterways—and it still does—but I know that any place that represents a challenge ultimately intrigues me enough to want to know how I can cope with it. Besides, I have been in the United States long enough to have visited every state, including Alaska and Hawaii, and was fortunate enough to be able to pack up at any time and live wherever I wanted.

The challenge of Houston was that it was different from any other city I had visited in the United States. Everywhere else I went, I was filled with nostalgia for the past. It seemed that I visited cities where the glory of living related to the past. Los Angeles, for instance, must have been the greatest city in the world when it was the center of the film industry—and then the city planners went mad and the automobile became more important than the comfort of people. Houston was a city of the future, belonging to the Age of Aquarius as well as the space age. Here I was convinced everything could happen and that it would probably take over from all other cities as the most powerful in America. I still think this is true. I would also remember it for the fact

18

that psychic forces nearly destroyed my entire family.

Both my sons and I love paintings, and throughout the years we have collected many beautiful ones. As soon as I arrived in our new home, I was anxious to get all the paintings on the wall. Once this is done, I always begin to feel that I live in a place; such things as normal household furnishings come second on my list of homely priorities.

As we unpacked, we began to talk about the strange circumstances that had brought three paintings into our lives just before we had left Florida. I had an urgent call from a lady living in Treasure Island, on the west coast of Florida, near Sarasota. Her heavy German accent was noticeable on the telephone; she was very distraught and asked for immediate help. Although time was precious, we drove to Treasure Island and had some difficulty in finding the address she had givn me. Most of the coastline had been devastated by a tornado, and when we finally found the house, it was in bad shape. Open walls revealed all the tragedy a major tornado can bring.

Mrs. T. owned what had once been a large motel on the beach, but all that was left was the shell of one unit. We picked our way gingerly to the doorway, skirting around large pieces of masonry and the broken remains of furniture. It was a pitiful scene, but dominating it was the large figure of Mrs. T., her face prematurely aged by pain and anxiety. I was accompanied by my lawyer, Mr. Ed Sigman, and his wife and my two sons, so we had some difficulty piling into the tiny apartment. But what an apartment! As a onetime antique dealer in Britain, I was immediately conscious of the value of the Dresden China, but most of all by the paintings—especially one

19

that was placed lengthwise on the floor behind a chair. It was difficult for me to force my attention back from the paintings to the woman, because she had called about a personal problem.

Mrs. T. explained that she was from Germany and then described her life there during the war at the time of the Hitler regime. As a Jew she had suffered considerably and twice escaped being sent to a labor camp. She lived for three years in hiding and helped several Germans escape. When one group of Germans invaded her village, she noted that a group of men were unloading several paintings into a requisitioned house. One day she managed to get into the house and discovered they were mainly paintings of the Renaissance period and obviously of high quality and value. Much later, when most of the Germans had left the village, she persuaded two influential townsmen to go with her to the house, and she removed three paintings.

Twelve years ago she and her husband emigrated to Canada, taking with them their personal possessions, such as the Dresden and the three paintings. Finally she came to the U.S.A. and bought a motel on the west coast of Florida. What troubled her was the long line of devastating troubles that had beset her. The premature aging, illnesses no doctor would diagnose, business deals that had gone wrong even though she had the reputation of being a good businesswoman.

At first I was inclined to think that most of the troubles stemmed from mismanagement, but this proved to be wrong. She was a highly intelligent woman. And although she had never been able to master the English language, she spoke good French, and my lawyer was also able to converse with her in

German. So between us we got a clear picture of her plight. What worried me was the ravaged look of the woman, and I remarked *sotto voce* to my lawyer that she looked as if she were possessed.

Anyway, we comforted her and offered advice, some of it practical from my lawyer about a delinquent partner and the insurance on the motel and some spiritual advice from myself. She seemed relieved that we had listened so patiently to her tale of woe and gradually we settled down on a more social basis, complete with tea and small cakes.

Only then did we begin to talk about the Dresden and paintings in her house, and she was delighted to know that I had a strong background in antiques and had been a professional valuer of paintings and antiques in Europe. We managed to drag out the large painting hiding behind the furniture, and my two sons held it up so that we could get a good view of it. Magnificent is the only adjective that could be applied to this painting; it glowed with the hidden fires of so many of the Renaissance pictures. It looked like a Raphael, and the subject was Persephone being snatched by Pluto, the god of the underworld. We admired all the paintings and duly left, feeling we had not only helped her mental state, but had been given a bonus of a wonderful experience, which any good painting can always provoke in me.

Stephen had majored in art in England and was especially interested in the Renaissance period, so the paintings were conversation pieces for several days. Then the phone rang; it was Mrs. T. She asked if I would try to find a buyer for one or all three of the paintings. Naturally I asked her what steps she had taken to sell them herself, and there followed many discussions about people who had seen the paintings. While I was convinced that the period was right for the painting, I was not convinced it was a Raphael. Like many of the famous painters Raphael was not averse to doing part of a painting and leaving students to finish the rest. I felt that Raphael might have had some hand in the painting, but against this was the fact that many of the professional people who had seen it had not grabbed the opportunity to buy it. After all, there is big money in art—especially anything officially attributed to Raphael. But the misfortunes that seem to have affected the entire life of Mrs. T. were always present in her dealings with members of the art world. Twice she was on the verge of a sale involving a large sum of money and special conditions that she should have the large painting authenticated—but each of the prospective buyers died suddenly.

To my surprise Mrs. T. asked me to take the paintings to Houston, where she was convinced we should find a wealthy buyer. In view of the value of the paintings, I asked my lawyer to draw up an agreement between Mrs. T. and myself. Mrs. T. brought the paintings over, Julian made wooden crates for them, and we carried them ourselves to Houston in the car rather than let them go with the rest of the furnishings in the truck.

Unpacking was a great adventure, and the questionable Raphael was put on the wall of our lovely dining room until we could find a suitable art gallery in which to display it. We found the gallery, but we never moved the painting because difficulties immediately arose about its insurance; it was safer left in the house because some member of the family would always be at home. Naturally I was anxious to get on with a sale, for the commission would be phenomenal. (I aimed to sell it as an oil painting of the Renaissance period.)

Among our friends were some very wealthy South American brothers to whom I had sold paintings before. They came to look at the painting and were totally fascinated. We discussed huge sums of money— subject, of course, to authentication. We agreed on a price, and I was prepared to travel to London with the painting and leave it at Sotheby's for every known test. On the day the South American brothers were expected to come to pay a deposit we waited in vain for their appearance. There was no phone call until late in the evening, when a friend rang up. I was petulant about the nonappearance of the brothers, and my friend was silent. Then she informed me that they had been killed in a car crash and dreams of making a quick fortune were eliminated, complete with all the horror anyone feels when tragedy hits on a personal basis. I began to think that there was something to the idea expressed by Mrs. T. that the paintings were bewitched, but I was not frightened. After all, such things were part of the mainstream of my own life.

In April of 1970 we had our first taste of psychic phenomena in the house. Stephen, my eldest son, slept in the master bedroom, which had its own bathroom. I slept in the middle room and Julian on the other side of the house. About two A.M. I was awakened by a noise, like someone dropping a piece of heavy furniture. It seemed to come from Stephen's room. I ran into the circular corridor, only to bump into Stephen, who had

23

heard the same noises, but thought they had come from my room, which was divided from his by the large bathroom. In a few moments Julian joined us and said he had dreamed a bomb hit the house.

We sat up for about an hour, not really worried about the incident, drank tea, and headed for our various rooms. Next morning, Stephen got up looking abnormally tired and complaining of a violent headache. Neither boy, normally devoted to the institution of eating a hearty British-style breakfast, was able to eat anything. By noon everything went back to normal and we thought nothing about the incident of the previous night. Everything in the house was in place, and there seemed no need to worry.

That night we went to bed late, but I woke up to hear loud noises coming from Stephen's room. It sounded as if someone were bumping furniture around, pausing for a moment, and then breathing heavily. I entered the room with Julian. Stephen was in his own bed, but it had been swung around by ninety degrees and in the process had grazed other furniture. What amazed me was that Stephen seemed to be asleep but his face was very red, and he was completely tied up in the bedclothes.

He awoke at the sound of our voices and was amazed to find that his bed had been moved. He thought we were playing tricks on him to wake him, but it is doubtful we could have moved the large bed, complete with a one-hundred-seventy-pound body in it. Stephen said he felt as if someone had tried to get into his bed, and so he had twisted the bed clothes around him so that whoever it was would have no clothes. We teased him about this, and went to bed again.

The next night I heard a crash and ran again to

Stephen's room to find him sleeping peacefully; nothing was disturbed. I decided to go to the bathroom and was horrified to find the place looking as if a bomb had hit it. Spare toilet paper, normally kept in the cupboard under the washbasin, was piled into the toilet; surplus supplies of cosmetics were scattered in the bath; and a bottle of nail polish looked as if it had been flung violently at the wall behind the bath. It was red and was dripping down the wall. I called the children, who could not believe their eyes. By now I was beginning to get the message that we were being psychically sabotaged.

We discussed the incidents with an old friend, Jinx Dobbins, who owned an interior-decorating business in town and was interested in psychic phenomena. She decided to come over to the house at eleven P.M. and, with us, would sit up and see what happened next. Jinx arrived, as always with her West Highland white terrier, Charlie (who made his own niche in history when he appeared in the Nieman Marcus catalogue, complete with tartan cap and scarf). Charlie was used to my three Siamese cats, but since one of them had produced kittens, they were not having their usual freedom of the house and were content to remain in my bedroom. We all sat in the dining room, overshadowed by the Renaissance painting.

Jinx began to shiver with cold, although it was a warm night, and we all felt a tremendous drop in the temperature. Charlie, normally very vivacious and full of terrier tactics, which include trying to give the impression that perpetual motion is a fact, suddenly began to whine and cringe with his tail between his legs. At the same time there was a frantic scratching at my bedroom door. I thought it was the cats, but as I reached the corridor I knew that my cats did not have the strength to create such loud scratching noises. Had I kept cheetahs or lions as pets, it would have been more understandable.

I was not even surprised to open the door quietly and see all the cats asleep in two baskets, Geisha with her kittens in one basket, Guisno and Daysha in the other. The scratching stopped for a moment and then seemed to move across the floorboards. Two of the kittens were flung from the basket into the air, landing with a sickening thud on the floor. Geisha leapt out to protect her offspring, but instead of retrieving them, she snarled and twisted around as if something were attacking her from the rear. I could only look on in a state of stunned inactivity. Finally Geisha retrieved her kittens, alternately growling and licking them. The room seemed quiet and I returned to the rest of the family in the dining room.

By then I realized something had to be done, and after some discussion we decided to hold a séance the next evening. Jinx said we ought to have another friend of ours, Marge Crumbacker, a journalist on the Houston *Post*, and her friend, Betty, a real estate broker. Everyone agreed to come, more as an idea to be helpful than to assauage curiosity. At the time I had no reason to associate any of the eerie happenings with the painting, but when we held the séance in the half-lit dining room, we received lengthy messages by trance and by automatic writing, and every one related to the paintings.

Now, although I am very friendly with Jinx, Marge and Betty, not too many of our conversations were wrapped around anything to do with psychic phenomena. Mostly we discussed aspects of our various professions. Marge Crumbacker and I were close to each other because we are both writers; Julian worked for Jinx in her interior-decorating business; and Betty and Stephen were linked because of their mutual interest in the expanding building program and architecture of Houston. At no time had either of my sons or myself talked to them about the paintings. All they knew was that I had many paintings for sale and that these three were to be sold on commission for a client in Florida.

Before the séance Stephen had set up a tape recorder, and Betty was armed with plenty of paper and pens so that she could record the session. Jinx has always been mildly interested in psychic phenomena; Marge was not particularly interested in it except from a journalistic point of view, but she fully understood that nothing was to be published. This was to be a quiet, personal session designed to enable the Leek family to have a good night's sleep.

We had laughed about the phenomenon of someone trying to get into Stephen's bed, complete with some ribald, typically Texan jokes about it, but everyone knew that we were now seriously trying to solve the mystery of what was causing havoc in our household.

The first shock came when Marge, whom we regarded as down to earth and matter of fact, suddenly dropped into a light trance and began to talk in a very guttural German voice. Whatever she was saying annoyed Stephen, who was also in a light trance, and the two had a great verbal battle, apparently about the paintings. The table began to heave up from the floor; crashes came from the kitchen; Charlie ran yelping out

27

to the front door; and all the lights went out. The two came out of their trance, and Stephen wdnt to check the fuses. Everything was intact, and lights reappeared before he touched the fuses. We lit several candles around Betty, hoping that she could continue to record whatever was said, but the tape recorder refused to work—all that we had recorded on it were a series of harsh noises and then nothing more!

Later that night we transcribed all the notes and we had the first clue that the paintings were a possible cause of the disturbance. A German girl who lived in 1830 wanted the paintings returned to her family. Stephen, normally very placid, had become very aggressive, throwing out instructions that the paintings had to be crated up and taken to a place of safety and that he was responsible for them. We all retired but not without some difficulty, for when the front door opened, Charlie, who rarely leaves the side of Jinx, just shot into the road as if all the hounds of hell were after him. Probably they were, but giving chase to the hell hounds were six very tired adults who finally corraled Charlie five blocks away. By that time he was his usual hectic self, wagging his tail and pleased to see Jinx.

Next morning I called Mrs. T. and told her I would like the paintings to go to a sale room for inclusion in the next Parke Bernet sale of fine art. She agreed, and I called the company, which sent a representative to the house. He was very impressed with the paintings, and we were already feeling happy at the thought of the departure of the paintings. The man from Parke Bernet called in another member of the company, who agreed that full tests would have to be done and he would let me know when the gallery could take the paintings. In the next week I called the gallery half a dozen times a day with no result. They were not prepared to take the paintings into their custody until mid-September. The alternative was to take them to London myself. I did not relish the thought of traveling with three delinquent paintings, but out of the blue came a request to send one of the paintings to an expert in Germany. We hastened to get it off, feeling it might lessen the activity by a third, but that was rational thinking, and we were not dealing with anything logical.

I put garlic and salt in the corners of every room, with a double amount in the bedrooms, said the age-old incantations for banishment of evil spirits, conjuring them to be gone in the name of the Mother Goddess and naming her by all her names, including Diana and Astarte. We seemed to enjoy a few weeks of peace. Charlie visited us and frisked around, annoying the cats, and the kittens grew up to be lusty, ferocious Siamese, the pride and joy of the household.

Then, in June, the mayhem started up again. I did a radio show from the house and talked about the hazards of being a writer, but I was unable to concentrate because of strange noises in the ceiling, which were upsetting the interviewer as well. That night Stephen was flung out of his bed and we thought he had a broken nose. The bed was swung around and almost upended by the window, the bathtub was flooded, and the room was a wreck.

We finally moved Stephen into Julian's bedroom and began the chore of tidying up the room, accompanied by snarls and grunts from the ceiling. In a strong, commanding voice I conjured whatever it was to be still, threatening to burn the house down if I had to in order to prevent the phenomenon from manifesting itself again. As dawn came the house was strangely silent.

The phone rang, and it was an old friend of ours in Los Angeles. Jim Newman has worked for years as a newsman. I first met him in Kansas City when we were working on a case of exorcism, and I was reminded of it. So far, I had done the banishing ritual, but my conversation with Jim reminded me that exorcism looked as if it were looming up in my own home. Jim said he was coming to Houston for a few days and wanted to discuss a film with me. It was on the tip of my tongue to invite him to stay with us when I realized that we could not expect even a dear old friend to go through the hazardous life we were now involved in. So we said we would put him in a nearby motel and he was very agreeable.

He was expected to arrive at the end of June, so we had a couple of weeks literally to get our own house in order. Every night we did a banishing ritual in Stephen's bedroom with varying degrees of success, but the noise and destruction lessened. Stephen, however, was not faring so well. He had lost thirty-five pounds and his good, athletic figure looked too spare to be healthy. He seemed to limp and lacked energy but was otherwise bright and cheerful and content to spend all his time doing research on the paintings. Every time I suggested sending the remaining two back to Mrs. T., he argued against it. We seemed to spend all our time spreading garlic and salt around the rooms and murmuring incantations, but it was worth the effort to keep the household on an even keel.

Just before Jim Newman was due to arrive, Stephen made up his mind to go to England for a month's vacation, and we were relieved to see him leaving; we hoped a month in the old family house with his grandmother would bring him back to better health.

Jim arrived. He loved the antiques, especially the paintings. We did not discuss the séance, and as I had arranged for him to meet many of our friends, including Jinx, Marge and Betty, I had taken the precaution of asking them not to mention the séance.

But if we thought everything macabre was behind us, we were mistaken. On the last Wednesday in June a picture came flying through the air and hit me on the head and the scratchings and howlings started again. But so did our energetic activities with garlic and salt; every inch of each room was fringed around with shredded garlic mixed with salt. I was spending more time going from room to room doing incantations than I was writing. Jinx was very consoling and hit on a bright idea. Her husband, Norman, is a big land developer in the Houston area, and responsible for recreating Pirates' Cove near to Galveston.

"One of Norm's houses is empty," said Jinx. "Let's all go to Galveston! I'll invite Marge and Betty, then you and Julian can come along and bring Jim Newman with you. We'll take two cars and be on the road at three o'clock on Friday, okay?"

It sounded great and I realized that in the six months since I had moved to Houston I could not count one day when I could say I had enjoyed the house that had seemed to hold so much promise of happiness. A weekend away from it would be a good boost to our jaded nerves. That night I had the pleasure of going from room to room, throwing out fearful insults to whatever spirits remained.

"See how you like it in an empty house!" I yelled defiantly. Not a creak or a single scratching noise replied, but I took the precaution of removing the large painting from the wall and locking it in the closet in my own room. So much for good intentions and hopes of a peaceful weekend in Galveston with people of whom I was fond.

Galveston was to be almost the Waterloo for the Leek family and their friends, but even if I could have guessed at the mad weekend that ensued, I would have reminded myself that Waterloo was one of the finest hours in the history of battles.

The British won, and when it comes to pitching my own strength against spirits, I feel akin to the Iron Duke of Wellington, who could never visualize defeat, much less concede to any enemy.

Someone has to deal with unruly spirits, and my own household was not going to continue to be a battleground for demented psychotic poltergeists. It is only now, in retrospect, that I realize that at that time I was incapable of thinking in terms of full exorcism.

It took a weekend in Galveston to bring that into focus.

Chapter Two

Nightmare in Galveston

At three o'clock we were ready to start off on our weekend in Galveston. Jinx brought her new Rolls-Royce, which seemed a good way to start on any journey. Julian took my Chrysler Imperial to pick up Jim Newman from his hotel. We teased him about traveling with the baggage car while Jinx, Marge, Betty, Charlie and I wallowed in the luxury of the Rolls-Royce. We purred our way through the hot humidity of Houston; I was learning that Houston, with all its amenities, does not have an especially good climate. Despite the air conditioning in the car and the bright conversation, I was longing to be by the water again and realized how much I missed Florida. Lazy days sailing on the lovely Indian River seemed to belong to the past, but I cheered myself up by thinking that I was getting away from our poltergeist-ridden house.

I knew the house was right on the beach, nobly built by Norman, and furnished with the impeccable good taste Jinx brings to all her interior decorating. She was elated at having brought off a contract to do a series of rooms at Howard Hughes' hotel, the Desert Inn, in Las

Vegas; the ambition of her life was to have her own Rolls-Royce and not have to borrow her husband's. We teased her and offered friendly sympathy, while Marge moaned about her ancient, but not yet antique, flivver, which miraculously got her to work but could not be relied on to venture anywhere outside the city. Betty slummed along with a new station wagon, generally accompanied by sets of window frames or other necessities to the building trade, for not only is she a realtor, but also one of the few licensed women builders. Three practical professional women heading for a quiet weekend in Galveston, chattering away like magpies and sensible enough to keep any personal problems to ourselves.

We entered Galveston and found the first veils of fog descending on the place as we stopped the car to go into a gift shop to buy magazines and newspapers. Lazing on the beach was firmly entrenched in the minds of all of us. We wanted to do nothing more energetic than stagger back to the beach house from time to time to sip a glass of champagne and nibble on strawberries, paté de foie gras and caviar. If you travel by Rolls-Royce, you may as well go the whole way first class.

Julian and Jim caught up with us and took Charlie along to inspect some palm trees. The first twinge of worry hit my head as I thought of my cats. We had arranged for a friend to go to the house each day to feed them, impressing on him that he should do this no later than five P.M. Even though we had had few ghostly incidents lately, we did not want to be responsible for exposing a friend to whatever was in the house.

The new beach house was, indeed, right on the beach at Pirates' Cove, a roomy place with high steps leading

34

up to it because it was built on stilts. We could just discern it as we rounded the bend of the estate, the fog having dropped to large filmy blankets, clammy and cold, as we stepped out of the cars and got ready to unload. Charlie raced up the steps, barking a welcome from the top; Jinx went ahead to unlock. The fog fascinated me, reminding me of Alderney cn the Channel Isles in the English Channel. I lingered behind with the menfolk, suddenly feeling reluctant to go up the steps into the house, but finally we all helped in humping and lugging picnic baskets and small suitcases.

I stood in the doorway and surveyed the scene. What I should have been admiring was the glorious decor, the brand-new velvet couches, the elegant kitchen, the handsome Swedish stove suspended from the ceiling with a fire already burning in it because Norman had thoughtfully called one of his men to get the fire going. From the first footstep into the house I felt the old gooseflesh feeling I always get before anything spectacularly psychic happens. It is not fear, because I have yet to be frightened by phenomena, but rather more a sensitive, delicate awareness of a yet-to-be-experienced incident. I was shocked to find myself feeling revulsion for the place, even though the rooms looked as if they were about to be photographed for inclusion in *Beautiful Homes.* I felt the tightening of my solar plexus as a waft of fetid odor hit my nose. No one else seemed to notice it because everyone was busy attending to the fire, exploring the place with ooh's and aah's or unpacking.

I was brought back to reality by Marge and Betty telling me that we were all on a disaster course. How did they know what I thought? But they were only referring to the fact that Jinx had threatened to cook the steaks, and we all knew Jinx rarely cooked. She could design a fine kitchen and look elegant as a model standing in one, but work in a kitchen was completely incompatible with the stylishly beautiful Mrs. Jinx Dobbins. Marge offered to cook; Betty begged to be allowed to do it, saying she knew how to break in a new kitchen better than anyone. Even Jim insisted he felt he could manage steaks and asparagus. But no—Jinx was determined to cook. We urged her on with instructions, advice, offers to help and yells when the steaks needed turning. There was no such nonsense as, "How do you like your steaks?" We got them all the same way: nicely charred on the top and raw underneath. We ate the lot, still teasing each other about this and that. I still felt a repulsion that I half understood but was reluctant to allow grow in my mind. Something unpleasant was hovering around and soon it would show itself.

After dinner, to my surprise, Jinx said, "I know Sybil is going to argue about it, but let's have a séance." She was right; I did argue about it because I never like séances, except for a specific purpose, and that night I could see no reason to have one. I knew she was completely serious, though, and no one else seemed to be arguing about it. Jinx rattled on, giving us a quick rundown of the area. (I gather that New Orleans pirate Jean Lafitte had once used the land as his base when he was in hiding.)

"Maybe old Jean will come through," said Jinx. "Wouldn't it be fun if he told us where he buried his treasure?"

I knew that the last person we could expect to make contact with us was the pirate. I tried a last-minute stand to prevent the séance but was laughingly overruled by my hostess and my friends.

Julian turned to me as we were preparing to seat ourselves around the table and said, "If you feel yourself going under, fight it," which seemed an odd remark to make, but by that time I was convinced it was not going to be the lazy weekend we had expected, and everything would ultimately add up to oddness.

We sat at the table, a modern round one with a central stem base, and quite heavy. Jim laughingly remarked that it would take a healthy athletic type of spirit to move this table. I suggested I would keep the record, but nothing happened except when I put my hands on the table, and then it began to heave and lurch around—but I was determined not to give in and sink so easily into a trance. On my right sat Marge; next to her was Jim, then Jinx; next to her was Julian; and Betty sat away from the table with pen and paper ready to take notes. The fire was burning beautifully and brightly, and the room should have been warm. We all began to shiver as some of the cold fog from outside seemed to invade the room. Charlie gnawed away at the remains of a T-bone steak.

After a hectic lurching of the table, which lasted for several minutes, Jim said, "Look at Marge!" She was staring, glassy-eyed, at the doorway and, in a voice unrecognizable as her own, shouted out, "Who are you? Get out!"

A black cloud seemed to swell up by the doorway and, growing in size, invaded the room, moving swiftly toward the table. Jim ducked his head, murmuring a four-letter word. The black cloud descended on everyone, starting with Julian and working its way around the table. It hovered near to me, but did not seem to touch me. I looked toward Betty sitting beyond the table. She, too, was untouched, but was sitting with a terrified look on her face, the pen and paper on the floor by her side.

I wanted to tell her not to be afraid, but was distracted by Julian, who slumped headfirst onto the table. I looked at Jinx, bolt upright in her chair, the lovely gray-green eyes sightless. Jim was clawing the air and screaming. Everyone was in a trance except me, and I had to fight back the desire to go under as I have never fought it before or since. Marge began to talk in the same nonrecognizable voice and Julian answered her, savagely snarling. Jinx was beginning to move away from the table, walking stiltedly. She turned around as she reached the door, raised her hand, and the sound of a shot from a gun rang out. Marge turned around, her face no longer that of a woman, but of a distorted, angry man. She, too, held up her arm as if firing a gun, and again there was the distinct sound of a bullet whistling through the air. By now everyone else was involved except Betty and myself; she cowered back in the corner in horror. I felt as if I were watching an Al Capone gangster film.

Rapid firing continued. Jinx fell to the ground and I hauled her back to the table. She blinked a few times and then came out of the trance, but only for a few minutes, then she slipped back again. One by one I went around to each of them, commanding them to return to normal, my throat drying up so much through lack of saliva that I thought I was choking. In my mind I knew I had to be firm and deliver each command to each individual. Marge and Julian were the most difficult to rouse, but finally made it and all leaned back on their chairs exhausted. I explained what had happened, but no one believed me.

Betty remembered enough to verify most of what I told them, and Charlie finalized it. Jinx missed him first, and we had to hunt through the apartment until we found him under the bed, nothing like his brave terrier self. Jinx carried him back to the living room in her arms; as they entered the door, he cowered and resisted entering. We all sat down at the table again, not with any intention of going ahead with the séance—we had all had enough of that. I noticed Marge was slowing her speech, and the glazed look was coming back in her eyes. I tried to snap her out of it by holding her shoulders and peering into her eyes in order to hypnotize her and at least have sufficient control over her so that she did not slip into another trance. It was too late.

"Look!" she said. "It's there again!" She pointed toward the doorway. A small, dark, filmy cloud hovered in the doorway and again began to burgeon so that it filled first the entire doorway and then exploded into the room.

Jim Newman leaped to his feet. "I'm going to get it!" he yelled as he headed for the door and the dark cloud. He had taken only a few steps when he fell to the floor as if someone had tackled him by grabbing his legs. He shadowboxed with some unseen force while we watched, inert with shock and fear. Then the attack on the legs ceased, and Jim raised his hands to his throat as if he were being strangled. I could see the color of his face changing; the neck and cheeks became swollen, and his shirt was half pulled off his back. I moved toward the writhing, fallen body of Jim. After some difficulty, I was surprised to get my voice back with plenty of strength and authority in it.

First the plea to the Mother Goddess for help; then the conjuration for the evil thing to leave the body of Jim.

> In the name of the Mother Goddess!
> Leave this man!
> I conjure you in the name of Diana!
> I conjure you in the name of Astarte!
> I conjure you in the name of Lilith!
> I conjure you in the name of Bridget!
> In the name of all good creatures,
> Leave this man! Leave this man!
> Leave this man! Leave this man!

I do not know how many times I intoned this incantation, but Jim finally stopped battling with the evil thing that had attacked him. Painfully he raised himself to his knees and then stood up. He is six feet four inches tall, weighs two hundred pounds and is in good physical shape; in sports it takes a tough guy to throw Jim Newman to the ground, but we had all seen him thrown and attacked and totally subdued by a superhuman force.

Afterward, in an affadavit, Jim said he felt as if an entire concrete wall had hit him in the legs, and he described a sensation as if heavy, burning claws were tearing at his flesh. When he reached the table and sat down, he pulled up each leg of his trousers—revealing ugly red marks. The same marks appeared on his chest and throat, and also on one shoulder. (For many days afterward he was a mass of bruises and was sore all over.) It seemed as if we were free of everything again, but in the confusion of attending to Jim, we had forgotten Marge, who was still glassy-eyed, her body taut, and hands extended like claws with the most awful expression of hatred on her face. I tried to pull her out of the trance, but nothing worked—and Julian was going off again!

They were staring at each other as if they were enemies instead of very good friends. Jinx and I hauled Julian over to the brand-new sofa, about six feet long, dominating the wall on the right side of the Swedish fireplace and left of the door. It seemed more important to concentrate on Marge at this stage, and the point of moving Julian to the sofa was to get him out of direct line of her gaze.

We had no sooner put him on the sofa and started back to the table to attend to Marge when a whole volley of shots rang out. It seemed that they came from every corner of the room. Jinx was so startled she slipped and I had to haul her back to the table, but I could see that she was already dropping into a trance. In anguish I saw that Jim, too, had faded out, and Betty was the same way. The expression on every face was completely different from the normal visage. Julian, a handsome, fair-complexioned boy, seemed like an old man, his face creased with wrinkles. Betty was sitting bolt upright on her chair but with her arm held out as if she had a gun. She pointed it at me and I quickly sidestepped out of her line of vision. Shots rang out; Jim fell off his chair as if he were dead. Marge was struggling to get out of her chair but seemed to have hurt her leg; she kept clawing at it with the same malevolent expression.

I was alone in a beach house in Galveston with my son and my best friends held in the grip of evil. Something had to be done or someone would get killed. I sensed that Julian was to be the target and I think at that moment I had all the instincts of a tigress about to defend her young, but I knew this basic maternal instinct would not be enough to save him.

Everyone in the room had to be exorcised! And I knew I had to get someone out of the trances so that they could help me. I started on Jinx, again and again intoning the conjuration to the Mother Goddess. Again and again—and yet again.

She moved, moaning a little, and the evil expression began to leave her face. The bloated cheeks were reduced again to their normal tension and texture. She came out of the trance, stretching her legs gingerly, blinking her eyes. When she could focus on the scene, she asked what was going on. I explained as quickly and lucidly as I could and impressed on her the need to be careful but to join me in whatever I did.

Then we started on Jim with the same incantation to the Mother Goddess, and it seemed to go on forever. Jim came out of the trance badly, almost crying with pain from his bruised and scarred leg. At last I got him in a sitting position and told him what had happened. Next Betty came out fairly well, but wanted to leave the room at once.

"You have to stay!" I told her. "I need all the help I can get. Just sit quietly there and visualize Julian and Marge as they normally are. And fight any inclination to go into a trance. Keep your eyes on me."

Jim called out, "Watch Marge—get her!" By then she had managed to get to her feet and was heading toward Julian. Jim and I intercepted her, but she hit out at us with ferocious strength.

"Kill him!" she screamed in her new guttural voice and there was no doubt of her intention.

Jim and Jinx held on to her as I backed away toward Julian, again conjuring the Mother Goddess loudly and firmly. Something in my mind was conscious of being very cool, knowing from long practice that I must not slur any words and so be able to keep some semblance of control.

The house was filled with a whirling wind, so strong that it almost blew us off our feet, but fortunately Jim managed to control Marge.

An indescribably sickening odor was in my nostrils, almost choking me, but I kept on with the conjuration. The fire, which had almost died away, suddenly burst into flames, which leapt out several feet from the stove, almost catching the bottom of my long dress. My body felt the attack of heavy clubs beating on me.

There was a tremendous crash. We turned around and saw that the couch on which Julian was lying was rising in the air. I yelled to Jim to hold on to Marge. The sofa turned right over so that Julian was trapped beneath it. On the other side of the room, chairs and side tables gyrated noisily. Julian and Marge were mouthing frightful obscenities at each other, but there was no time to consider the niceties or wonder why they were saying such things.

I continued with the conjuration, interrupted many times by Julian. Then Jim almost slipped as the weight of Marge pressed against him. She suddered convulsively, but to my relief, after a few moments, supported by Jim and little Jinx, she spoke in her normal voice.

"I'm going to faint," she said—but she did not. I stopped the incantation and directed my attention to her, commanding her to return to normal and help her friend.

She revived, but did not seem too steady on her legs, so Jim guided her gently to a chair. Then she saw Julian.

"My God," she said. "What has happened? Was there a tornado?"

I explained to her as briefly as possible that some evil force was in the place, and we had to get rid of it and that it was important to help Julian.

It took all of us to move the sofa from him, revealing him as a large, bloated mass on the floor—but his face was not quite so evil. We lifted him onto the sofa again, but he seemed terribly heavy—much more than his usual 160 pounds. It took the strength of four of us to heave him up, and we were not helped by the heavy unseen hands clawing at our arms.

Julian was breathing heavily, blue eyes open but unseeing. We surrounded him and yet again I started the exorcism. On and on, again and again. I could feel the others getting tired, so from time to time I stopped to encourage them to concentrate.

"Help me!" I cried. "If you don't, he is lost forever!" They seemed to understand and revived as I once again started the incantation. Julian moved a little and raised his hands toward me. I gripped his wrists firmly and half lay over him so that I could focus on his face. From time to time his hands struggled to free themselves from me, but I felt that if I let go, he would slip away again.

The swelling in his body went down, his color returned to normal, and he moved his head.

"Don't take any notice," I said to the others. "Keep concentrating! He's not out of it yet."

44

Julian forced my hands down so that they rested on my chest. His fingers seemed to be clawing as if to reach something. I realized he was trying to reach the antique crystal I always wear around my neck on a long silver chain. I looked at Jinx without stopping the incantation; she understood what was in my mind. Gently she moved the crystal so that it was within reach of Julian's hand. He gripped it so hard I could feel the chain cutting into my neck. Mentally I thanked my lucky stars it was on such a long chain, because I was able to maneuver my head so that the chain was released from me. As soon as he held it in his hand, so firmly the knuckles shone like polished white stones, he seemed to be relieved. His body relaxed; his face was the same as it always was, but he was breathing heavily.

"He's all right," Marge said, and went to get a towel to wipe his face, gently dabbing away at it. He turned and gave her an impish grin. "What goes on?" he asked. It was too soon to tell him. I released my hands from his wrists but he still held on to the crystal, looking at it in surprise.

"That's funny," he said. "I had a dream and in it I knew I had to get your crystal from you, but something tried to keep me away from you." It was the understatement of the year! But explanations had to come later; we were all exhausted. Jinx was pale and limp, but Marge seemed to be her usual practical self, running to the kitchen and making coffee. Jim was occasionally groaning with pain. Betty was silent as a mouse, her thin face tired, strain lines showing under her eyes.

Julian swung his legs off the sofa so that he sat upright, his eyes darting around the room. "When did the bomb hit?" he asked, as he looked at the disorder in the room. "You sure had a ball while I was asleep."

Carefully he stood up, wincing as he did. "I feel as if a steam roller ran over me," he said. His legs, wrists and chest were badly bruised.

We told him what had happened and he took it very well. We asked him how much he could remember, but fortunately all he could say was that something hit him and that he remembered hearing shots fired.

Marge remembered nothing. We sat up for several hours, and I told them all that had happened. Marge was frankly disbelieving until she looked at the bruises on Jim and Julian. Everyone else felt we should leave the place at once, but I thought it was all right to stay since I felt the atmosphere was better than when we had arrived. Whatever the horribly evil presence was, it had certainly gone now. Jinx went to the door and said we could not leave anyway because the fog was too thick. Betty was frankly nervous about staying, but we soothed her. That night the girls all slept together on the floor and Julian in the bed in one of the bedrooms. We were not brave enough to stay much longer in the living room.

After a private conference in the kitchen Jim and I decided we would stay awake all night in the living room, but neither of us wanted to use the comfortable sofa or even the chairs, so we sat on the floor and talked about the devastating events of the night, amazed to find that it was only four A.M. We seemed to have lived through a dozen nightmares, which is more than anyone should have in any given night. We kept watch on the others in the bedroom and were relieved that they all slept like babies.

About ten A.M. the next morning we decided that our

weekend in Galveston was a fiasco and we did not need to take a vote to decide to return to our respective homes. Even Charlie was delighted to go and didn't try to chase the seagulls, which he usually loved to do.

On the way home we discussed the events of the night. Marge was worried because she says she does not go for "that occult business." As far as I could remember we seemed to have got ourselves in a time warp and somehow had got back into a period of time when gun battles may have taken place on the land where the house was built. Marge said she would check it all out, which she ultimately did, and we discovered that in the days of prohibition, a gang of Chicago rackateers came to the area and had many running battles with local bootleggers, each striving for supremacy in order to take control of the area. The explanation made nearly everyone happy—except Jim and myself.

Looking ruefully at his bruises, he said, "I reckon we were all possessed. Whatever got me was something evil and had more than superhuman or superspirit strength, and Julian and Marge were different people."

I could not help but agree with him. I believe we had two forces against us that night in Galveston. I think we did, indeed, slip into a time warp, but I also believe that through the the ground had built up a powerful force of evil that was just waiting to be released. Our own psychic awareness had released it and enabled it to live again in the bodies of Marge and Julian.

"It's a good thing you kept your head," Jim said to me. "Wonder what would have happened if you hadn't kept going with that incantation of yours?"

I could have told him very bluntly, but refrained

47

from doing so. There would have been a murder that no one could have explained.

Once we were back in Houston, and before Jim and Julian had seen the last of their bruises, we all agreed that we must prepare a statement about the nightmare in Galveston and have it signed legally by a notary. This was done, but none of us likes to refer to the weekend that got away from us or our own battle with the tremendous terrifying forces of evil. Sometimes we laugh about it, but we all know that any memories we have of that terrifying night are sealed in our subconscious, with luck never to emerge.

Sometimes I feel angry about the whole affair. When we read or hear of anything tragic—a murder, a rape, a mugging—we never think they can happen to us. We sympathize with the victims and that is as far as emotion goes. We have the same attitude toward possession. It is something that happens to other people, but that is one of our biggest mistakes.

It could happen to *you*—and if it does, I hope someone is there to perform an exorcism.

It was only when we reached our home in Houston that I began to wonder if we had been responsible for taking some of the evil of that place with us to Galveston. For months we had been exposed to tremendous psychic attacks, building up week after week. At one séance we had been instructed never to leave the paintings without someone in the house; the spirit of the nineteenth-century girl had been firm about it. Well, we had left the house unattended, even though I had hidden the main picture. On our return the house was serene and beautiful for the first time in

48

many months, as if a huge black cloud had been lifted from it.

A huge black cloud?

Like the one that had appeared in Galveston?

Well, whatever it was had dispersed now. The house felt good, smelled good, and *was* good—but I was not going to take any more chances.

Forgetting such things as adequate insurance and prepared to battle with transport people, I had the paintings crated and returned to Mrs. T. in Florida. Stephen returned from England looking very well and happy. He was back to his old weight again, and life settled down for the Leek family in Texas.

Chapter Three

Evolution of the Devil

In considering possession, we are faced with discovering what or who is in possession of a living body, using it as a home and trying to function through it. Although the Greek word *daimonia* is usually translated as "devils," the word "demon" is more correct. There is only one devil (from the Greek word *diabolos*) and his name is Satan. Demons are spirits, emissaries of Satan, and so numerous as to make his power practically ubiquitous. Such demons are capable of entering and controlling both men and beasts, and often seek embodiment—without which they are unable to fulfill their potential for evil.

The devil did not emerge from a trap door accompanied by a loud burst of thunder, as Gounod described Mephistopheles' entrance in his opera, based on the alchemist Dr. Faustus. The image of the devil and his personality was slowly formed in the mind of man during the course of millennia long before the beginning of Christianity. It is a safe assumption that the devil has always been with man, and he has kept pace with his evolution, changing his personality and vices to meet those in all arenas of civilization. However, the devil, or Satan, has never deviated from hating humility and purity and so becomes the natural antagonist of God, the Supreme Being who is the epitome of purity and humility. It is an amazing, if unpleasant, fact that Satan has always received as much attention as God in every age and civilization, despite the organization and structure of numerous religious groups. The prize, of course, is the spirit of man, and for this God and Satan are in eternal combat. The odds are on the side of God, the personification of all that is good, because the teachings of most churches have been designed to save man from going to the devil. But all men cannot follow the rigid rules set out in the dogmas of the churches, so many fall by the wayside. The devil is not too particular; a spirit is a spirit, and if it were possible to obtain statistics, I have no doubt that we would find that the inhabitants of heaven and hell are not too far apart in numbers.

First of all, however, one must believe in heaven and hell as actual places—which I do not—but I certainly believe that the forces of good are always opposed to the forces of evil. God in his mythical heaven has an entire entourage of angels anxious to help him in his work; Satan in his subterranean realms of mythical hell has his emissaries, the demons. Both angels and demons have been heavily categorized by theologians, with Michael being the archangel and Satan having an entire army with regimental names such as Beelzebub, prince of the legions; Astaroth, the grand duke; and Sargatanas, the brigadier major. Every angel and saint in the Christian world has its function and influence over mankind. Saint Jerome is in charge of lost causes, while Saint

Anthony helps to find lost possessions. Every angel and saint has its counterpart in the hierarchy of Satan. If Saint Anthony finds lost possessions, you can be sure that Raum, a demon, had a part to play in causing possessions to be lost, for he is the demon very much concerned with theft.

The advent of the devil has always caused great controversy among theologians: If God created everything, then He had a part in creating evil. It follows, then, that Satan in some sects is considered to be as much a part of God as man, "who was made in the image of God." This is heightened by the accepted fact that Satan was a fallen angel, formerly known as Lucifer, the Prince of Light and Son of the Morning. It was a long fall from favor to become the adversary of God and ruler of the nether regions. The chances of salvation of the devil are biblically very slight, but he is not entirely without hope. According to one of the sacred books of Persia, the *Bun Dehesh,* the devil will be saved. This prediction finds its counterpart in the writings of Saint Jerome, who believed that the apostate angel will recover his original condition and man will be able to enter again into the paradise from which he was driven forth.

Saint Jerome, the saint of lost causes, is surely the ultimate optimist, but he is not alone in believing that Satan will be rehabilitated. The same statement is made in the Cabala, those mystic, secret writings of the Jews. In this work Samael, called the angel of poison, will lose half his name: when the first syllable *Sam* (the Hebrew word for poison) is eliminated, there remains *Ael,* and that is God. Thus, we have the eternal prediction again that good will always survive and vanquish evil. The

EVOLUTION OF THE DEVIL

trouble is that succeeding generations have not whole-heartedly thrown in their weight on the side of God, and the collection of spirits by Satan has continued, so that all that remains of religious predictions is hope. Man can sustain his built-in desire for self-preservation only if he retains hope; destroy that and he is unable to cope with distressing circumstances, even those inflicted on him by Satan. In cases of possession, the exorcist must always have hope that he will succeed; it is this that bolsters up self-confidence, the other ingredient for success.

For several years now I have asked various cross sections of people what they think about Satan and how they got their first idea that he existed. Everyone told me that the introduction to the adversary of God is found in the Old Testament with the story of the serpent tempting Eve when she lived in the Garden of Eden with Adam. On consulting the Bible, I can see no basis for this at all, although Genesis tends to explain the origin of good and evil according to the ideas of mankind in very remote ages.

Chapter III of Genesis is probably the most dramatic, debatable and discussed passage in the Bible. Yet within the story of Adam and Eve there are numerous anomalies, contradictions and masses of repetition. On Genesis, other religions divide; each has sought its own interpretation or drawn it from an earlier source.

Very few stories in the Old Testament are peculiar to the Christian Bible; we can find their counterparts in earlier cultures of Assyria and Babylonia. The story of Adam and Eve is no more an exception than the story of the Great Flood.

To go back to the idea that most people are

introduced to Satan through Genesis and the Garden of Eden, I find that there is no mention of which fruit Eve picked. We presume it was an apple, but the Bible says: "she took the fruit of the tree and ate." If we concentrate on the tree that produced the fruit, we may begin to see it as the same Tree of Life so well known to the Assyrians that they used it on their seals, complete with two upright figures, one male and one female. If we accept a loose translation of the Latin word *pomum* as meaning apple (actually, *pomum* means fruit), then we find this mentioned in the Song of Songs (VIII:5).

If we are unbiased enough to admit one mistake in Genesis, then it is easier for us to see another that is important in the context of this book. This brings us to the usual idea that the introduction of Satan comes in the form of the serpent in the Garden of Eden. Again, there is nothing in Genesis that logically allows us to assume the serpent is the devil or any other spirit of evil in disguise. The serpent in Genesis is just a serpent, whose action in inducing the first couple to infringe on a prohibition of God brought one major church to acknowledge temptation as the foremost sin, for which all mankind thereafter must suffer. But the serpent belongs to many ancient cults and religious sects, in existence long before the time of Moses, the law-giver. It was not until many years after the birth of Jesus Christ that serpents began to disturb the world and become associated with the devil. Their previous history was of a godlike status, as the serpent was in Phoenicia. Like the worship of the sun, those religions following the cult of the serpent became the enemies of the new religion of Christianity. In the ensuing rivalry the serpent was relegated to being a creature of evil connotation, which later became associated with the devil. Through many ages and civilizations, the serpent was thought to be capable of interchanging values, an attribute we now assign to the devil.

For hundreds of years after the Bible was written the snake varied between being the bearer of great revelations and the incarnation of evil. The Gnostic sect of the Nassenes, both early Christian sects, reversed the account of the serpent in Genesis, seeing him not as the devil but as the Messiah. To the Gnostics, Ophites and Nassenes, the serpent was the chosen instrument to fight against Yahweh, the black god who introduced evil to the world. The idea of the serpent as the Messiah gave rise to the curious rites of the Eucharist of the Serpent, described by Saint Epiphanius, Bishop of Constantia on the Isle of Cyprus. The bishop died in 403, but described the rites in his treatise called *Panakeion.*

> They pile up loaves of bread on a table, then summon the serpent they keep as a sacred animal. His basket is opened, he comes out, goes onto the table, writhes among the loaves and transforms them into a Eucharist. Then they break the bread among themselves and distribute it to the communicants. Each one kisses the serpent on the mouth, for it has been tamed by incantation and they prostrate themselves. Thus the supper consists of making the logos [truth] present in the serpent's body. By contact, the serpent consecrates the bread. He gives the holy communicants the kiss of peace and carries to God the thanksgiving of the faithful.

The fundamental Christians will see this as heresy,

but the treatise was written by a bishop, who presumably saw nothing terrible in the writing of an event that was well known among Assyrians and Babylonians, both people of great antiquity.

We find many more references to the devil in early Hebrew literature, where he is given many personal names—including *both* Satan and Lucifer, which is not a deviation from the Christian idea that Satan and Lucifer are one and the same. The name Satan means "adversary" in Hebrew and originally meant merely an opponent, not necessarily a supernatural one. The Philistines, for instance, were afraid that David might become their satan, or adversary (Samuel I:29). Later an angel appears who is called the Satan, and he is a member of God's court, but his duty is to act as prosecutor, stating the case for man against and before God.

In the book of Zechariah (III) a high priest is judged by God and "the Satan is there to accuse him." When we reach the book of Job, written sometime after 700 B.C., the Satan is still there, but is now glimpsed as a highly obnoxious type, and it is this personality of Satan that is still in existence.

The Satan of Job tests how man's actions match his life-style. Let me remind you of the Satan's conflict with Job. He challenges Job's belief in God, saying that it is easy to praise God when all is well; but given a strong dose of misfortune, the Satan wagers, Job will renounce God. Then God has the children, servants and cattle of Job destroyed, but Job is faithful and refuses to renounce his God. To complete the punishment, the Satan inflicts Job with horribly painful skin diseases, but still he remains faithful. From that date the Satan becomes a less-than-pleasing figure, but we should not lose touch with the fact that according to ancient writings, he started his career as a useful official of the heavenly court of God before he became the master of evil and the adversary.

The development of Satan as a malignant being and the supreme enemy of God was probably influenced by Persian Zoroastrianism. Palestine was part of the Persian Empire until 800 B.C. The followers of Zoroaster believed in rival gods of good and evil. In their version of the creation the world was made by the good god but was invaded by the evil god Ahriman-Sheitan and his legion of fiends. It took many centuries for the Jewish and Christian religions to sort out the status of the Satan and the status of God. Gradually all good was attributed to God and all evil to supernatural powers, with the Satan as the arch-adversary. The first and only use of Satan as a proper name appears in the Bible in Chronicles One, Chapter II:

> And Satan stood up against Israel and provoked David to number Israel.

In the Jewish Book of Jubilees all evil actions are credited to an angel called Mastema, whose name translates as "hatred."

In the Greek Bible Septuagint, the name of Satan is implied by the word Diabolus, meaning "he who disunites and causes hatred." The Septuagint also uses the word *daimon*, meaning "demon" and implying a divinity of an inferior but not necessarily evil order. In the apocrypha books known as "The Testaments of the Twelve Patriarchs," an evil angel named Belial becomes

Satan, Prince of Deceit. Not only is he the adversary of God, but also the enemy of man. Belial rules "the kingdom of the enemy," waiting for those who sin to fall into his clutches.

The exit of Lucifer from heaven is described in Isaiah, Chapter XIV. The reason for his expulsion is pride; he loved himself to the exclusion of all else. Since the rejection by God was eternal, so must be the subsequent punishment of Lucifer. But another version of the fall of Lucifer is described in Genesis, Chapter VI, which describes how "the sons of God saw that the daughters of men were fair; and they took to wife such of them as they chose."

There is a parallel story in a Jewish book which was not included in the Old Testament, the first Book of Enoch. This version is much more descriptive, but essentially the same in content. Angels of the order of Watchers, the sleepless ones, lusted after the daughters of men. They took them as wives and taught them magic, astronomy, botany and the manufacture of weapons. The children of the angels and the mortals were monsters who killed each other. God slaughtered the monsters, and the archangel Michael imprisoned the delinquent angels in the valleys of the earth until the time came when everlasting fire would consume them.

So now we have lust as one of the reasons for Satan being loosed on the earth to torment mankind. Every known evil then, and in all future time, could safely be attributed to Satan and his legion of demons, and by the first century after the birth of Christ, it was natural enough to think of the serpent in the Garden of Eden as the devil. Always lusting for human souls, Satan as Prince of Deceit, master of all known vices, was everywhere, ready to ambush men, tempting them to sin and dragging their spirits to reinforce his own domain in the underworld, which became known as hell. Only by the aid of God could man escape from the devil, and as the personality of the devil grew blacker, so the shining light of the godhead increased.

As the building of churches succeeded the building of temples, there was no lack of artistic endeavor designed to show the world what the devil and his demons looked like. In the great cathedrals of Europe his sinister presence can be seen everywhere in the shape of gargoyles, whose faces express every known emotion. Bats' wings on some of the gargoyles remind us that Satan was once an angel. In statuary the favorite depiction of Satan was a gargoylelike head, complete with horns, set on the body of a goat with a tail and cloven hooves. It is interesting to note that in England and Scotland, the last strongholds of the ancient pre-Christian religion, there is not a single artistic work showing Satan as a goat. There are plenty of depictions of his infernal lordship expressing all the vices known to mankind: lust, pride, envy, greed, and particularly sensuality. The devil has been the inspiration of many works of literature—notably as the great rebellious but romantic titan in John Milton's *Paradise Lost*.

In every age the devil has had faithful adherents to worship him, and Satanic cults all over the world have found no shortage of recruits. Many of the followers go willingly to the grottos and shrines to worship the devil. As the Prince of Deceit and the great tempter of men, he has no need to apply ethics to fulfill any promises, and man is—and always has been—demanding A daemonibus what he thinks he wants, not necessarily because he needs it. Desires of all kinds are part of man's basic animal nature, and if a high priest or priestess of the devil promises something in the name of the devil, there is always the hope that it will be achieved. Sometimes it is, but the high price paid for attaining desire through the devil is a man's spirit.

Today we live in the greatest scientific age in history, but the Church of Satan, organized by Anton La Vey, known as the Black Pope of San Francisco, is never short of recruits. It is not easy to obtain statistics, but I personally believe that "Pope" La Vey has something like a million followers in the United States alone. Attitudes toward the devil range from contempt, fear and a compulsive desire to seek evil for the sake of evil. His personality is whatever a person wants to see within the framework of his own life. To some he is another human being, a neighbor or even a relation, but endowed with all the vices the seer is afraid of. To others he belongs to folklore and fairy tales, but is as real as Saint George, Cinderella or even Jack of beanstalk fame. Once we admit that he exists in some form or other, through our own thoughts we give him substance, and so he thrives and walks in our midst. Where our thoughts of the devil are, so will our experiences be.

He has a convenient role to play, however, for by comparing all the evils laid at the foot of Satan, so we are able to place all that is good before the feet of God. Man prides himself on his free will, but unfortunately he overrates his ability to use this free will. Satan becomes the whipping boy for many of us, and sometimes absolves us from taking full responsibility for our own actions.

"The devil made me do it!" says a famous television star, and the words have become famous enough to be used as a catchphrase in many an American home. The trouble is that the catchword has more substance in it than the memory of a popular television show. We can find examples in every newspaper, where those accused of some especially obnoxious crime will plead that someone or something made them do it. The implication is that some force outside themselves—something supernatural—made them commit the crimes. On a broader scale we find a generation of middle-aged religious people who believe the devil and his demons have persuaded their children to leave home or get into trouble.

Without the image of Satan and his legions to act as scapegoats for mankind, we would find ourselves in the position of having to live very different life-styles, and be forced to accept responsibility for all the actions we take. Given a choice between good and evil, we find it difficult to go all out for good and eschew evil, despite the guidelines set down by the orthodox churches. This is probably much more of a phenomenon than possession. But there is always hope for those who become possessed. Satan, the devil, and all his demons have their own mortal enemy: the exorcist.

Chapter Four

Demonology

Demonology is the study or doctrine of demons. It includes the legion of demons, of which Satan, the arch-devil, is the leader. In form and meaning demonology has an obvious analogy with theology, the science or doctrine of God.

The great thirteenth-century Dominican doctor, Albertus Magnus, said of demonology: *A daemonibus codocetur, de daemonibus docet, et ad daemones ducit.* (It is taught by demons, it teaches about the demons, and it leads to the demons.)

Anyone studying demonology should first be able to sort out facts from the vast literature that is tainted with errors and, second, be sufficiently sure of himself that he, too, will not be taken over by the very demons that interest him

It is necessary to study demonology not only in context with the Christian religion, but also in relation to other cultures and religions. Only then can we gain any clear idea and appreciation of how demonology has influenced human history. Through human history we also see the impact on the religious, moral and social life of people within these cultures.

The constant recourse to incantations and magical practices has to be studied with an unbigoted mind. Many incantations and practices that flourished in the past seem to have disappeared, but there are others whose recorded origin may be traced to comparatively modern times. For demonology belongs to the past, the present and the future, flourishing among widely diverse cultures and is equally congenial to primitive and civilized societies.

In the primitive cultures, innocent and remote from science and civilization, we find constant evidence of a fierce belief in evil spirits. Attempts to propitiate these spirits and avert their wrath are not consigned entirely to folklore, but are part of everyday life. All spirits were at first conceived of as the souls of dead men, and from this aboriginal animism there was a gradual development of elaborate systems of mythology, angelology and demonology.

Safe in the sophisticated atmosphere of many of the cities in the United States, we are apt to forget that rude forms of worship are still found among primitive peoples throughout the world. Yet these forms of worship have a link with modern cultures and at many points find some counterpart in the pages of biblical scripture and Catholic theology. Devil worship is not a thing of the past but is right here in our midst. The great religions have taken the prevalence of devil worship into account as they devised their dogmas and rites.

Assyrian and Akkadian Demonology
Some idea of the antiquity of demonology can be gleaned from the Bible and other classical writings, and that idea is reinforced by evidence that there was a

universality of beliefs and practices concerned with demons. The main evidence comes from the deciphering of the cuneiform hieroglyphics, which opened the way to a study of the vast literature of Babylon and Assyria.

Frequently attention has been directed to the monuments left behind by past civilizations. With regard to demonology, some of the Assyrian monuments are of special importance. Apart from the public and official cult of the "twelve great gods" and their subordinate divinities, the Assyrians had a secret religion of mystery, magic and sorcery. These religious texts together with a mass of talismanic inscriptions on cylinders and amulets, prove the presence of a second religion organized to accept and perpetuate the presence of a demonic leader of a vast horde of demons.

The antiquity and importance of this secret religion, with its magical incantations and acceptance of evil demons, may be gathered from the fact that by order of King Ashurbanipal, his scribes made copies of great magical works, which have been preserved in the priest school of Erech in Chaldea. These works consist of three books. The first contains incantations, conjurations and imprecations against evil spirits. These cuneiform books are written on clay tablets and each tablet has come down to us with the title "Tablet No.—of the Evil Spirits." The ideogram is expressed as *kullulu,* meaning "accursed" or simply "evil." There is also reference to *limuttu,* meaning "baneful one." Other references to evil spirits are called *ecimmu* or *udukku.* One special class of these spirits was the *sedu,* or divine bull, commonly represented in Assyrian monuments as .

a man-headed bull. (The name *sedu* is probably the source of the Hebrew word for demon, but it should be rememberd that *sedu* can also mean a beneficial spirit or a teaching one. The good spirits of one nation frequently show up as evil spirits to members of rival nations. The old gods of one age become the devils of another.)

IRANIAN DEMONOLOGY

One of the most remarkable demonologies can be seen in the Avesta, the sacred book of the Mazdean religion of Zoroaster. Unlike the secret religion of the ancient Assyrians, Zoroastrianism still exists in the Parsi community. It accents much more clearly than the Assyrian religion the constant war between evil and good, between darkness and light, the battle between the good God, Ahura Mazda, and Anro Mainyas, sometimes called Ahriman, the evil one. The good God has a hierarchy of holy spirits; Anro Mainyas, demon of demons (*Daevanam Daeva*), has legions of lesser malevolent spirits.

The original meaning of the word *Daeva* is "shining one," and is derived from a primitive Aryan root *divi*, the source of the Greek *Zeus* and the Latin *deus*. There seems to be some significance to the fact that in its original context of "shining one" *Daeva* has a link with Lucifer, which meant Prince of Light at one time. Both *Daeva* and Lucifer at a later date became synonymous with "devil."

There is also a similarity of sound in the modern Persian *dev*. Looking at the likeness in sight and sound, it is probable that both words have a common origin, except that we also know that the word "devil" comes from *diabolus*. One can only wonder if there is a missing link between the Persian root and the Sanskrit word *deva*.

There is a noticeable difference between the demons of the Avesta and the devil in Christian theology. This is free from the dualism of the Mazdean system and yet allied inasmuch as each recognizes that good is always challenged by evil. The holiness and faithfulness of Zoroaster when he is attacked by Anro Mainyas and his demons brings to mind the numerous trials of the saints under the assault of Satan and his legions. The story of the temptations of Zoroaster is contained in a portion of the Vendidad, the largest book of the Avesta. It is sometimes printed as the Vendidad Sade, which means something that is "given against devils" or the *antidaemoniacus*.

JEWISH DEMONOLOGY

After the elaborate and well-documented demonology of the Assyrians and Persians, the sacred books of the Jews are much less explicit in their category of evil spirits. We find a great deal about the angels of the Lord, the seraphim and cherubim and other good spirits who stand in attendance before the Lord or who minister to men.

Although the mention of evil spirits is slight, the existence of demons is not entirely ignored. In Job, Satan appears as the tempter and accuser of the just man. In Kings, Satan incites David to murder the prophet. In Zechariah, Satan again is the accuser. There is also mention of an evil spirit who comes to false prophets, and Saul is afflicted and possibly possessed by an evil spirit. The activity of demons is shown in the work of the magicians of Pharaoh. And Lamia represents the original Lilith, a female spirit of darkness who, in Hebrew legend, is the demon wife of Adam.

The Book of Tobias is not included in the Jewish Canon, although originally written in both Chaldean and Hebrew. Here we find the demon Asmodeus, and he becomes a prominent figure in later Hebrew demonology. Asmodeus is very much the nonhero of the Talmud, and some of the strange tales about him are reminiscent of *The Arabian Nights.* In fact, the rabbinical demonology of the Talmud and Midrashen are far removed from the sobriety of most canonical writings.

In comparison with the demonology of other nations, Jewish demonology has a distinct character of its own, a relic from the beliefs and ideas of the chosen people long before they came into contact with the Persians and Babylonians. There is very little borrowing from the sources of alien systems, and the rabbinical demonologists used subtle and ingenious methods to establish their demons. Isaiah furnished a mysterious night female called Lilith as the demon wife of Adam and the mother of demons. This implies that the "first father" contracted a mixed union with a being of another race and begot children other than human. It also upholds the contradictions in Genesis VI:2, which tells how the sons of God "took to themselves wives of the daughters of men."

The Jewish demonology sees the air as full of demons that become the cause of many diseases. It was thought that men should guard their mouths lest, by swallowing a demon, they might be afflicted with some deadly disease. We have a relic of this today when we yawn and cover our mouths with a hand. This is acceptable as good manners, but originally covering the mouth was a means of preventing devils from entering into the body. When we sneeze, it is inevitable that someone says, "Bless you"—and in ancient times this was said with deep meaning and sincerity. With the chance of demons in the air, the quick intake of breath after a sneeze might also result in an intake of demons.

It is remarkable that the old superstitions of Jewish demonologists present a close analogy to the present theories of modern medical science. The air, as we know now, is full of microbes and germs; by inhaling any of these living organisms, we are capable of receiving disease into our systems.

DEMONOLOGY OF THE EARLY CHRISTIAN WRITERS

The air was certainly full of dangerous demonologies in the early days of the Christians. Men were able to adopt doctrines that held God responsible for everything and denied the right of divine creation to the devil. There are some sects that say the devil cannot exist. The principal source of biblical demons is the historical books of the New Testament.

According to Luke VIII:30, the demon is capable of entering into man as a second personality, using his body as a house—and so we get evidences of possession. According to Matthew XV:22, demons torture man, driving him to places against his will. On its own, the demonology of the Bible is not complete without reference to the demonology of Assyrians, Persians and Jews, for it is here that we find the source of so many of the Bible stories.

In the New Testament the demonic powers are

represented only as spirits, not flesh and blood. They can assume any form, even appearing as angels of light (II Corinthians XI:14); they dwell in ruins (Revelations XVIII:2), in tombs (Mark V:1), and especially in the desert (Matthew IV:1 and XII:43). Instead of direct reference to the devil and demons, we find numerous other names suggestive of evil, such as satyrs and he-goats. Mention of Lilith comes in Isaiah XXXIV:14, and she is sometimes called night hag or screech owl.

Despite all the variations and contradictions, the multitudinous systems of demonology all have something—if not everything—in common. So the demonology of Christianity owes much to the Jewish and Greek demonology, which in turn draws on Assyrian demonology And this goes back to the animism, the belief of evil spirits taking the form of animals.

The majority of Christians accept the belief that the devil exists in many forms and has lesser entities who pay homage to him and do his will. From the cradle most Christians are brought up within the framework of moral, ethical and religious concepts of good and evil, of God and his adversary, the devil. The Lord's Prayer, said by most Christians sometime during their lifetimes, exhorts the lord to "deliver us from evil." But no one has been able to answer the question asked by the Gnostics: "Whence comes evil?"

It may be pertinent to think that anything outside the conscience of any man is evil. In Christian demonology the devil sinned by trying to usurp the functions of God, but to the dualist the devil was identical to an ultimate type of God. Without the evil instincts of Judas, there would have been no crucifixion and no New Testament. The devil becomes relative to the individual with as many conceptions of him as there are of God. Perhaps the devil personified by Satan is the darker side of each man's nature, and there is a bit of the devil in every living human being. In cases of possession the evil forces overrun the good.

In considering the question of demonology in terms of Christianity, the modern definition of a demon as a devil or malignant spirit is the result of a long development. We should not confuse "demon" or "devil" with the words as used by ancient writers, since they often used such words as interchangeable variations on the general theme of demonology. The original demons and devils are today blanketed by general designation, but once they had distinctive. names and many interchangeable characteristics. A demon can be broadly defined as an anonymous god, a personification of one or another of certain vague and less identifiable powers that exerted influence along with the major deities.

In Homer "demon" and "god" are completely interchangeable in connotation, as with the Iranian term of *daeva*. When Homer means a noxious or bad spirit, he says so very clearly as in his *Odyssey* V-396, X-64, XXIV-129; and the Babylonians and Assyrians speak of both good and bad demons.

AMBIGUITIES OF HISTORIC DEMONOLOGY

In the Old Testament, *Saimon*, the Hebrew equivalent of "demon" in the original sense, was *Elohim*, commonly translated as "god." When Rachel declares at the birth of Naphtali that she has been wrestling with her sister Leah, she has also been wrestling with Elohim (Genesis XXX:8). What she means is that she has been struggling with her as if possessed by a demon. When Balaam makes his ability to prophesy dependent on an encounter with an Elohim (Numbers XXII:38; XXIII:3), what he envisages is also possession by such a being.

The power that is represented as a personal being can also be represented as a personal influence or spirit. For this reason demons and spirits usually exist side by side in the primitive mind as alternatives to the same thing. In the Old Testament we find a considerable distance has been achieved from the primitive, and there is a merging of the concept of daimon as a god or a demon, and we find a gradual movement toward accepting that the spirit emanates from a daimon. So in one idiom the impulse to prophesy is attributed to an encounter with an Elohim or daimon as in Numbers XXXIII: 4; we find the contrast in Numbers XXIV:2 that it is the *spirit* of a daimon that alights on an individual. In the same way sickness described in the Bible as seizure by a daimon is also said to be produced by the evil spirit of a daimon sent by Yahweh (I Samuel XVI:15; XVI:23).

Guidance through danger in one idiom is portrayed as the work of a personal guardian angel, a daimon, as in Exodus XXIII:23 and XXXII:23, while in Isaiah XXXII:15 and Psalms CXLIII:10, such guardianship is by a spirit.

I recognize that the word "spirit" is used in two senses and both are important in considering cases of possession. There is the notion of spirit as identical with breath, and since breath leaves the body at death, the primitive mind concluded that it is but the physical manifestation of something that can exist independently of it. This implies that it simply takes up temporary

71

lodging within the body as its vital principle and thus determines its personality. This, in turn, gives way to the idea of disembodied personalities which spirits—as alternatives to daimons—really are.

But the word "spirit" also carries with it the meaning of wind, and the idea that spirits operate on human affairs arises also from the analogy of winds that blow where they will, wafting either good or evil toward men. We often hear the expression "winds of fortune," but it is more specifically described in the ancient Near East by the Akkadian expressions "good wind" or "bad wind." In this sense it is meant to express either a blessing or misfortune. There is also a widespread belief in the Orient that all diseases are borne by the winds.

With the development of monotheism, the idea of a single cosmic deity superseding that of a pantheon of controlling powers, we find that daimons and spirits become subordinated. The central figure becomes a single god, but one who has ministers or angels. However, they also coalesce into a single "holy spirit," which emanates from the single god. The holy spirit then represents the totality of his regenerative powers, serving to diffuse his personality in the world of his creation.

We now come to the essence of demoniac possession. Viewed from the standpoint of religious psychology, demonism represents the externalization of human experience. Moods, emotions, impulses, feelings, and sensations—even physical conditions that might otherwise be described as obtaining autonomously *within* man—then become portrayed as outer forces working *upon* him. Aspiration becomes inspiration, ecstasy or rapture, that is, a state of being "seized" becomes

72

revelation or insight. Emotion becomes "immotion," something that is projected out of the self—an invasion rather than an escape. In the vernacular of demonism, all such experiences are represented as visitations, that is, as actions of an external force rather than as internal psychic states. Terror is not something issuing from man's inner self but something by which the inner self is seized. Disease is not an organic disorder but is brought on by a demonic hand; in short it is a demonic assault.

When we speak of someone as being "love struck," "awestruck," or "stricken by disease," we are unconsciously employing the essential language of demonism, with the demon the assumed striking force. There is considerable ambiguity in speaking of "a troubled spirit" rather than "the spirit that troubles." This particular ambiguity is very evident in the Bible, where it is never absolutely clear whether the spirit envisaged is that which operates or that which is operated upon.

The word "demons" is used as a generic term in the early versions of the English Bible, denoting objects of pagan worship. Subsequent translations use the word "demon" to convey the idea of evil spirits or bogeys. Demons have survived as figures of speech long after they ceased to be figures of belief; an example is the word "gremlin." Gradually specific demons emerge from ancient Near Eastern sources and we find parallels to them in other cultures; some are mentioned in the Old Testament. The ambiguity occurs because most of the specific demons occur in the most poetic passages of the Bible, and in some cases can only be construed as figures of speech. In fact, locating a demon as a consistently evil spirit is not easy to do.

In the apocryphical texts, during the postexilic and

intertestamental periods, there is a greater clarification of demons. The conception of demons, as of angels, was enormously influenced by the infiltration of Iranian ideas. The principal influence was to turn demons into devils, transforming anonymous gods into definite and distinct forces of evil. The clear function of the new devils is to inflict misfortune and disaster on man and to seduce him from a well-ordered life. The favorite candidate for the role as leader of all devils and demons was Satan, already familiar from the Book of Job and the prophesies of Zechariah.

Today the existence of demons as agents of every known evil is more or less taken for granted, and they continue to be regarded as the ministers of Satan. Their aim is a final confrontation with the forces of righteousness, apparently unconcerned about the threat of punishment by eternal fire. Against these evil forces there is the authority of the godhead, and in the Christian religion, Jesus Christ, the son of man. Once help is invoked from the godhead or the son of man, evil spirits are expected to obey. This is the most important attribute to conventional religious exorcism. The expulsion of devils or demons by invoking against them the superior name of God is standard practice in exorcism by priests. This is because the name is not regarded as a verbal appelation, but an integral part of the personality and imbued with the power and virtue of the personality. The only names of demons mentioned in the New Testament are those of the prince of devils himself: Satan, Belial, Beelzebub.

The devil by any name is bad luck to anyone to whom he directs his attention, and he is well served by his legion of lesser demons; but master and slave-demons are linked in open desire to possess a human being, mind, body and soul, and function through it in order to perform evil acts before any confrontation with an exorcist takes place.

Demons are the psychic muggers, rapists, murderers, thieves and destroyers, and are not discriminating in their choice of victims.

Chapter Five

Possession in the Bible

Man is in various ways subject to the influence of evil spirits. By original sin he is said to have brought himself into "captivity under the power of him who thence had the empire of death." Even though redeemed by Jesus Christ through his death by crucifixion, man is still the target of the devil and subjected to numerous violent temptations.

> For our wrestling is not against the flesh and blood, but against principalities and powers, against the rulers of the world, of this darkness, against the spirits of wickedness in the high places.
>
> EPHESIANS VI:12

But the influence of demons goes still further because the body of a man can become the home of a demon and he becomes what we call "possessed."

We know that in ancient pagan nations cases of diabolic possession were numerous and frequent. In the Old Testament, however, we have only one instance, and this occurs in the first book of Kings. An evil spirit from the Lord troubled Saul.

The life of Jesus Christ, subsequently recorded in the books of the saints of the New Testament, is full of instances when he cast out devils. The phenomenon of possession becomes common in the New Testament. Sometimes the victims are deprived of sight and speech, sometimes afflicted in ways not clearly specified, and in a great number of cases, there is no mention of any bodily affliction beyond the possession itself. The possessed are sometimes gifted with superhuman powers.

The Bible can always rise to dramatic phases, and the first occasion on which Jesus met a demoniac, that is, a — X possessed person, is indeed highly dramatic. Early in His public life, the scene took place in the synagogue at Capernaum.

> And in the synagogue there was a man who had an unclean devil, and he cried out in a loud voice: "Let us alone! What have we to do with Thee, Jesus of Nazareth? Art Thou come to destroy us? I know Thee who Thou art, the Holy One of God."
> And Jesus rebuked him, saying: "Hold thy peace and go out of him." And when the devil [having torn or convulsed him—Mark I:26] had thrown him into the midst he went out of him and hurt him not at all.
> Luke IV:33–35
> Mark I:23–26

There were other occasions in the gospel record of a day spent by Jesus at Capernaum. He healed the sick

> and the devils went out from many, crying out and saying: "Thou art the Son of God!" And rebuking them He suffered them not to speak for they knew that He was Christ.

77

Luke IV:41
Mark I:34
Matthew VIII:16

Saint Mark tells us in his gospel (III:11–12):

> And the unclean spirits when they saw Him, fell down before Him, and they cried, saying: "Thou art the Son of God." And He strictly chared them that they should not make Him known.

One of the most colorful and dramatic incidents of possession occurred when Jesus landed on the eastern side of the Lake of Genesareth, in the country of the Gerasenes. The account by Saint Mark contains a wealth of vivid detail, while the same incident is reported with more sobriety by Saint Matthew, and with meticulous precision by Saint Luke.

> And He went out of the ship, immediately there met him out of the munumehts a man with an unclean spirit, who had his dwelling in the tombs, and no man could bind him, not even with chains. For having been often bound with fetters and chains, he had burst the chains and broken the fetters in pieces; and no one could tame him. And he was always day and night in the munumehts and in the mountains, crying and cutting himself with stones.
>
> [Saint Luke adds to this description that the man had gone unclothed for a long time.]
>
> And seeing Jesus afar off, he ran and adored Him. And crying in a loud voice he said: "What have I to do with Thee, Jesu the Son of the Most High God? I adjure Thee by God that Thou torment me not." For He said unto him: "Go out of the man thou unclean spirit." And

78

He asked him: "What is thy name?" And he said to Him: "My name is legion for we are many." And he besought Him much, that He would not drive him away out of the country.

[Saint Luke substitutes the word "abyss" for country.] And there were there near the mountain a great herd of swine feeding. And spirits besought Him, saying: "Send us into the swine, that we may enter into them." And Jesus immediately gave them leave. And the unclean spirits, going out, entered into the swine, and the herd with great violence was carried headlong into the sea, being about two thousand feet, and were stifled in the sea. And they that fed them fled and told it in the city and in the fields. And they went out to see what was done; and they come to Jesus, and they see him that was troubled with the devil, sitting clothed and well in his wits, and they were afraid. And they began to pray to Him that he would depart from their coasts. And when he went up into the ship, he that had been troubled with the devil, began to beseech Him that he might be with Him. And He admitted him not, but saith to him: "Go into thy house to thy friends and tell them how great things the Lord hath done for thee, and hath had mercy on thee.

Probably of all the gospel stories this one gives us the clearest characteristics of devilish possession in a human being. The demons create a morbid type of madness, but also have enough intelligence to recognize Jesus; they even plead with Him and compromise by saying they will go into the swine. No sooner do they enter the hitherto innocent swine than the superhuman power of the demons causes them to panic and rush to destruction. One of the common and noticeable things about possession today is that the demons within can be

79

abusive or coyly resort to flattery. And I never yet encountered a demon who did not like to have conversation with the exorcist, almost as if there is enough intelligence to reason that the exorcist may possibly be forestalled in his work and induced to reply. It always seems like a great ploy to hinder the expulsion—which must come—but the demons want to savor every moment of being in possession. Such conversations can unnerve all but the truly dedicated exorcist.

One of the most famous cases of possession in the New Testament is again clearly described by Saint Mark (IX:14–38). Jesus found a possessed young man at the foot of the Mountain of Transfiguration. He was also a deaf mute and showed symptoms of what we would now identify as epilepsy. The sickness of the boy confused the apostles and all who knew him.

And coming to His disciples, He saw a great multitude about them, and the scribes disputing with them. And He asked them: "What do you question among you?" And one of the multitude answering said: "Master, I have brought my son to Thee, having a dumb spirit; who, wheresoever he taketh him dasheth him, and foameth and gnasheth with the teeth, and pineth away; and I spoke to the disciple to cast him out and they could not." Who answering them said: "O incredulous generation, how long shall I be with you? How long shall I suffer you? Bring him unto me"; and they brought him.

And when He had seen him, immediately the spirit troubled him; and being thrown down upon the ground, he rolled about foaming. And He asked his father, "How long time is it since this hath happened to him?" But he said: "From his infancy"; and often times hath he cast him into the fire and into waters to destroy him. "But if Thou canst do anything, help us, have compassion on us." And Jesus saith to him: "If thou canst believe, all things are possible to him that believeth." And immediately the father of the boy, crying out with tears, said: "I do believe, Lord; help my unbelief." And when Jesus saw the multitude running together, He threatened the unclean spirit, saying unto him: "Deaf and dumb spirit, I command thee go out of him and enter not any more into him." And crying out and greatly tearing him, he went out of him, and he became as dead, so that many said, "He is dead." But Jesus, taking him by the hand, lifted him up and he arose. And when He was come into the house, His disciples secretly asked Him: "Why could we not cast him out?" And He said to them: "This kind can go out by nothing but by prayer and fasting."

Jesus did not always need to be confronted by a possessed person in order to drive out the demons. When a Syrophoenician Gentile woman came to Jesus and fell at His feet when He visited Tyre, she besought His help for her daughter. Jesus said to her:

"Go thy way; the devil is gone out of your daughter." And when she was come to her house, she found the girl lying upon a bed and that the devil was gone out.
Mark VII: 25–30

In some cases in the New Testament there is not a description of possession but rather of infirmity attributed to the influence of Satan. Such is the case of the deformed woman in the synagogue.

And He was teaching in the synagogue on their sabbath. And behold there was a young woman who had a spirit of infirmity eighteen years; and she was bowed together, neither could she look upwards at all. When Jesus saw her, he called her unto him and said to her: "Woman thou art delivered from thine infirmity." And He laid His hands on her and immediately she was made straight, and glorified God. And the ruler of the synogogue, being angry that Jesus had healed on the sabbath, answering said. . . . And the Lord answering him said: "Ye hypocrites, doth not every one of you on the sabbath day loose his ox or his ass from the manger and lead them to water? And ought not this daughter of Abraham whom Satan hath bound, lo, these eighteen years, be loosed from the bond on the sabbath day?"

Luke XIII:10–17

Skeptics often prefer to refer to the healing ministry of Jesus and choose to ignore the fact that in all cases of healing the deliverance is effected under conditions and circumstances that clearly differentiate from merely curing a disease. In those times, of course, the plight of sick people was commonly associated with the influence of evil spirits, but Jesus, in his healing and casting out of demons, is very precise. The epileptic was cured—but precisely because the unclean spirit was cast out. The woman with the bent back was "delivered from her infirmity" after having been "bound by Satan for eighteen years."

I do not think we can presume that in His attention to the possessed, Jesus was only accommodating himself to the ignorances and prejudices of his contemporaries, but rather that He knew that evil spirits could wrack mankind and that in many cases sickness or infirmity

82

was only a spin-off from the original evil of being possessed.

It is illogical to think that the whole idea of possession rests only in imposture or ignorance. The examples of possession in the Bible are primarily a matter of historic reference. The cumulative force of centuries of experience cannot be dismissed lightly since the main evidence can be found in the action and teachings of Christ as revealed in many passages of the New Testament. Natural diseases and possession are, in fact, clearly distinguished from each other by the Evangelists. "He cast out the spirits with His word; and all that were sick were healed" (Matthew VIII:16) or, alternately, "They brought to Him all that were sick and that were possessed with devils, and He healed many that were troubled with diverse diseases; and He cast out many devils" (Mark I:32, 34).

This distinction is more clearly expressed in the original Greek version of the New Testament. Saint Matthew did not believe that lunacy and paralysis were often mistaken for possession, for he says:

> They presented to Him all sick people that were taken with diverse diseases and torments and such as were possessed by devils and those who had palsy, and He cured them.
>
> Matthew IV:24

The circumstances affecting various cures by Jesus points in the same direction. Ordinary diseases were dealt with quietly and without violence. But this was not so with the possessed; the evil spirits passed into lower animals with drastic results, or the victim was cast to the

83

ground and the evil spirits, "crying out and greatly tearing him, went out of him and he became as dead." Most of the healing techniques of Jesus were explained by the laying on of hands, but this is rarely the case when there is any indication of possession. In healing per se, hands were laid on before the cure was effected; in possession Jesus would help a person from the ground after the possession was eliminated.

The Jews of the time regarded certain manifestations as coming from a diabolic source. If, therefore, possession were only a natural disease, then it is surely logical to assume that Jesus would have remarked on this and, since His mission on earth was divine, would surely have done all he could to eliminate anything erroneous. He was always quick to proclaim any false doctrine, as He did when His apostles spoke of the sin of the man born blind. The disciples asked, "Who has sinned, this man or his parents, that he should be born blind?" Here there is evidence of prejudice, which Jesus replied to with a simple truth: "Neither hath this man sinned nor his parents but that the works of God should be made manifest in him."

On no occasion did Jesus correct his disciples' expressions on the subject of demonic possession, and He frequently took up a position on His own on this point and defended it, as we see when we read about the Pharisees who accused Him of driving out lesser devils by the power of Beelzebub. It would have been quite easy for Jesus to remark that possession was merely a disease. Instead He told them that the devils do not cast each other out but are driven out because they have come up against someone stronger. Jesus speaks of the devil and of possession by the devil as realities.

So we have within the healing ministry of Jesus two distinct types. First there are cases in which exorcism and healing are combined. Secondly there are cases such as deafness, dumbness, blindness and paralysis unaccompanied by any mention of the devil or demon. The cures for these are brought about by expressions of the utmost kindness and compassion, very different from the imperious, authoritative and threatening cures by exorcism.

> And they came to Bathsaida; and they bring to Him a blind man, and they besought Him that He would touch him. And taking the blind man by the hand, He led him out of the town, and spitting upon his eyes, laying his hands on him, He asked him if he saw anything. And looking up he said: "I see men as trees, walking." After that again He laid his hands upon his eyes and he began to see and was restored, that he saw all things clearly. And He sent him into his house.
>
> Mark VIII:22-26

There is no mention of casting out a devil here, merely symbolic gestures.

The gospels present possessions accompanied by various types of neuroses, but they also present pure and simple cases of neurosis alone. Today it is a constant mystery to many renowned theologians that medical men are content to explore cases and rely on the idea that there is only a neurosis to contend with. We often ignore the fact that true diabolic possession is accompanied sometimes by mental and nervous disorders. The transcendental causes are completely ignored and so many people go through long periods of

85

unnecessary suffering before the idea of exorcism takes root.

In His lifetime Jesus told His disciples how the evil spirit acted when cast out, but He also exhorted His disciples against glorifying in the fact that the demons were subject to them. He also conferred positive powers on his disciples "over unclean spirits, to cast them out and to heal all manner of diseases and all manner of infirmities" (Matthew X:1, Mark VI: 7, Luke IX:1). Note again that a clear distinction is made between casting out unclean spirits and healing "all manner of diseases."

Before His ascension into heaven Jesus enumerated the signs that would proclaim the truth of the revelation, instructing His disciples to preach to the world:

> In my name they shall cast out devils; they shall speak with new tongues. They shall take up serpents; and if they drink any deadly thing, it shall not hurt them; they shall lay hands on the sick and they shall recover.
> Mark XVI:17–18

If healing by laying on of hands is considered a miracle, then we may have to think of casting out of devils in the same terms.

Jesus was able to see the difference between disease or neurosis and possession—which brings me to a point of wonderment that so many of our modern clergymen and medical men refuse to face up to: the fact that possession is not something that can be brushed under the carpet or relegated to the absurd, the ignorant or the superstitious. It was a fact at the time when Jesus walked the earth and has been with us ever since.

To a certain extent I can understand the point of view of medical men much more than I can that of clergymen. The theological literature contains many reports from the various councils that legislated on the proper treatment of the possessed, and that parallel with the public penance for catechumens and fallen Christians, there was a course of discipline for the energumens, also. Finally, the church established a special order of exorcists.

The literature of the Middle Ages is also rich with the reports from numerous councils discussing the matter of possession. Laws were passed and penalties decreed against all who invited the influence of the devil or utilized it to inflict injury of their fellow men. Students of this phenomenon should read the papal bulls of Innocent VIII in 1484, Julius II in 1504, and Adrian VI in 1523. Powers of exorcism were then conferred on every priest of the church and the phenomenon was accepted by all true Christians. There are also records of criminal investigations in which charges of diabolic possession formed a prominent part. To name only a few works available to the general public, there are the following:

Des Mousseaux, *Practique des demons,* Paris, 1854

Theirs, *Superstitions*

Constans, *Relation sur une epidemie d'hysterodemonopa-thie,* Paris, 1863

Pauvert, *La Vie de N.S. Jesus Christ*

Raupert, *The Dangers of Spiritualism,* London, 1906

Lepicier, *The Unseen World,* London, 1906

Miller, *Sermons on Modern Spiritualism,* London, 1908

In the twentieth century it has become a policy to deny the possibility of possession. We presume—erroneously, I believe—that there are no evil spirits any

87

longer in existence or, if there are, we think we can ignore them. Alternatively, we may even believe that no evil spirit has the power to influence the human body. Then when we think we have solved the whole thing, we find obscure reports of possession and subsequent exorcism taking place right up to the present time. It seems that it would be the ultimate in optimism to believe that God would not allow evil spirits to exercise their powers. All around us we can see examples of sin and sorrow in the world, and if this line of thought is continued to its logical conclusion, then these things also would not be tolerated by God. The sun, moon, and the stars shine on the just and the unjust, on the righteous and the not so righteous.

Chapter Six

Hostages of the Damned

For thousands of years all forms of madness, grossly abnormal behavior and sometimes physical disease have been explained in terms of possession of a living body by a discarnate spirit—generally an evil one. Accounts of possession are found to have many traits in common, although possession may occur in any place in the world and is indifferent to the sophisticated veneer of civilization. The history of possession culled from antiquity varies very little from possession in modern times. The interior dispositions that pave the way for possession show themselves by physical, emotional and intellectual signs, which all come to a head when the possession is complete.

The physical signs generally come first, with changes in the body and facial structure. The about-to-be-possessed looks like a different person and is often unrecognizable by friends and relations. As the possession progresses, there is a great emaciation of the body, although the stomach, like the stomach of a person suffering from severe malnutrition, is distended. The organic functions are badly affected by spasms, and bowel movements are frequent, with smells as disgusting as a thousand sewers. Urination is frequent, as is vomiting. There is a general foulness about the body, which, of course, is accentuated by the bowel movements and vomit. Often the victim will use his normal bodily functions to express dislike or hatred of someone else.

The victim is in obvious anguish, writhing and contorting his body and exhibiting a variety of facial expressions registering extreme hatred, terrific pain, and a feeling that something is inside him clawing away at his entrails. All too often the victim experiences pain from blows on the tender parts of the body, especially the nape of the neck and spine.

Frequently what appear to be brand marks made by a hot iron will appear on the skin, mostly on the stomach and chest, and sometimes the marks will take the form of recognizable letters, even messages and numbers. Noticeable changes occur in the voice, with a wide range of tonal qualities. The vocabulary is extended to include the most devastating obscenities, alternating with erotic sentences. In fact, any language that will shock normal society finds its way into the mouth of the victim.

Accompanying the obscenities there is always aggressiveness and superhuman strength; the victim can inflict physical harm on anyone who comes near him and especially on anyone who has a good reputation or any aura of spirituality. It seems that one of the most satisfying experiences for demons is shocking an audience; the term diabolic laughter applies very well in this case.

That the victim himself suffers, there is no doubt; the distension of the body makes him feel as if one or more small persons were inside him. He feels constant torture, together with cramps, convulsions and the desire to inflict pain on someone else.

Probably the worst aspect of possession is that the victim knows some evil entity is acting, speaking and working through him, and there is nothing he can do about it. The sense of inadequacy is cruel, even when it appears to a normal person. We have an example of this in a man who is impotent; he knows it and also knows that he is inadequate as a man, unable to achieve the function necessary to produce the life force. Consequently he, too, suffers side effects of a physical, intellectual, spiritual and mental nature.

A possessed person has a depraved appetite—if he has any appetite at all—and will deliberately eat offal and other disgusting things as if he is determined to shock anyone who is near, but even without an audience, there is a yearning for food no one else would consider eating. While the physical signs upset onlookers and cause distress to the victim, they are nothing compared to the anguish caused by the emotions.

The physical signs, being tangible, are easily recognized. But emotion is an intangible quality, and it is in the realms of the intangible which even this highly scientific age seems unable to appreciate, much less cope with. Of course the emotional signs can become the source of neurotic and psychotic illnesses, which can be approached by medical attention, but in the case of a person genuinely possessed there is never any satisfactory relief.

One of the most terrifying effects on the emotions is that of guilt, whether it is real or self-inflicted. Long before the possession takes place, the obsession of guilt

91

is often there and feeds the evil power. The patient feels that he was born to suffer, while others believe that only through pain can his personal guilt, real or imagined, be expurged. This is why certain people with strong but bigoted religious ideas produce the greatest number of possessions by evil forces. The normal happy-go-lucky inhibited native is not so often subjected to evil possession as are those living in sophisticated civilizations. Possession in less civilized societies generally takes the form of deliberate possession in order to achieve some form of healing or to obtain prophetic utterance. The fundamental Christian, raised on a strict diet of "Hell, fire and damnation," is a ripe subject for evil possession because he is obsessed by fear for his own salvation as well as frequent reminders that he is a "miserable sinner." Naturally not all fundamentalists are likely to be possessed because demonical possession can be retarded or eliminated by a sense of true spiritual awareness, the very quality half the world is lacking, while the other half seeks it through various paths of enlightenment.

While we can assess the misery and torment of the physical body through possession, we can never be sure of its effect on the emotions because emotion covers a lot of ground. Aggression, tenderness, pride, humility, greed and generosity, gluttony and abstention, love and hate all have an emotional connotation. In possession the first things to be eliminated are the emotions and qualities we regard as virtues.

Accompanying cases of possession is extreme cold, which is very noticeable to anyone entering the room of a possessed person. The victim, too, feels the cold, but at the same time feels as if he is literally being roasted in hell. The coldness can sometimes take the form of a high wind that blows through the room and is capable of doing damage in addition to causing extreme fear in those who experience it. Every discomfort known to humanity can be experienced, and the intensity increases as the possession becomes more complete.

The ultimate result from so many attacks should logically be death, but this is not the end product at all. Few people have been known to die by being possessed, although death has been known to occur soon afterward, even after an exorcism has taken place.

The reason I believe this is because the victim, after exorcism, generally experiences no memory of the possession or, indeed, of the exorcism, but the subconscious is known to retain memories of past events, pleasant and unpleasant, and is not discriminating when it brings them to the surface in dreams and nightmares. Therefore, it seems likely that if a once-possessed person commits suicide, some memory of past events is tossed up from the turgid realms of the subconscious and is sufficient to trigger the idea that death is the only way out—a possible escape route generated by the victim's fear that he may have to go through similar torment in the future.

The occupying demons do not seem particularly interested in the death of the victim because the body becomes their host, a place to hide and feel safe while manufacturing their diabolic plots against the good of mankind. It is always amazing to realize how much the human body can stand; it can be deliberately violated even without possession, or it can be subjected to horrible tortures inflicted by other beings, but no torture known to man can ever be so bad as that

93

inflicted by a demon using a human body as its hotel. I am sure that if the victim had any choice, he would choose death rather than possession, but one of the functions missing from the victim is his free will and his reasoning ability, which gives him a special place in this world above all other living things. Deprived of reason and will, it is no wonder that the possessed is often described as an animal, evil-visaged, evil in intention and capable of functioning through the throbbing, increasing intensity of the pure evil within him. If love can motivate a man to achieve all that is great in life, so evil—as strong as the forces of love—can bring about the downfall of a man and those associated with him.

Phenomena of many kinds always accompany possession, and poltergeist activity is kindergarten stuff compared with the damage a possessed person activated by all the forces of evil, can do. Doors are often heard slamming, footsteps or animals clawing away at woodwork, drums beating and loud cries like those of a hundred banshees wailing are some of the phenomena experienced. Loud noises and anything that can bring discomfort seem to be inevitably linked with possession. Objects traveling through the air, the mixing up of food in the kitchen, faucets turning themselves on are also part of the diabolic action.

One of the most disconcerting types of phenomena is the ability to read minds and anticipate action. This is why, when exorcism is discussed—away from the actual presence of the victim—there is generally an intensified outburst of unpleasant activity. The demons, while enjoying the attention and the discomfiture of humans, also realize their limitations, and spiritual activity designed to dislodge them makes them alert to creating a terrifying atmosphere in order to upset those who are dedicated to their dissolution. It is difficult for anyone who has witnessed cases of possession not to be frightened; loud noise, obnoxious odors, obscenities can play havoc on even the most hardened types, and the demons are well aware of this.

It is not unusual for those inhabiting a human body to have a sense of humor, but it is always designed ultimately to discredit or cause discomfort to anyone nearby. All human weaknesses are exposed in their raw, virulent ugliness; insults, obscenities and eroticisms are directed to those who normally would not be exposed even to mild words about such intimate subjects as sex and personal life. The gift of prophecy is not really a gift when it is activated by demonic forces, and most of the prophecies are designed to produce fear. Since fear of death is the dominant fear in most people, the threat to kill followed by some villainous attempts at choking or beating is enough to make all but the most devout and devoted people leave a person possessed by the devil or any of his legion of demons.

Absurd and exhilarated remarks are bantered around with demonic gusts of laughter, alternating with questions loaded with ambiguity. The more an observer, subjected to abuse, shows fear, the more pleasure the demons get from their attacks. To some extent an observer will take some of the torture from the victim, and it is mostly when the possessed is alone that the demons stir up their fiery claws to drag at his entrails and scar his body with lacerations. The most skeptical people, who think possession is something that belongs to the past and has no place in modern life, will often say that such wounds are inflicted by the victim himself.

Anyone who has seen lacerations, bruises and such things on the body of a possessed person will know this cannot be true, especially when oversize claw marks appear. Slight scratches may be a different thing, but in true possession everything is exaggerated, every bruise is the ultimate in bruises, every gash and laceration comes in king size. Even in cases of extreme madness it is logical to assume that it is not too easy to carve four to six inches of letters into the stomach or the back.

Temporary possession can occur during dreams or nightmares but is rarely as dramatic or horrible as anything inflicted during genuine full-time possession. The intimate connection between the visions of dreams and the hallucinations of the insane gives rise to the old but popular idea that the demons of nightmares were also the cause of madness. Ancient doctors saw the origin of madness in chronic nightmares and especially in epilepsy, sometimes called "the falling disease" because its victims fell down frothing at the mouth. Today we know that neither nightmares nor epilepsy is the source of madness, but the knowledge of wise medical men still does not diminish the agony undergone by people suffering from various mental diseases and epilepsy. The same can be said of psychosomatic symptoms; the patient feels extreme pain and discomfort, but he is told that because his doctor cannot diagnose what is wrong, he is imagining the pain. But a pain is a pain is a pain when you are on the receiving end of it. The source, even if it is in the intangible emotions, is just as real as the pain inflicted by a knife wound or the gripping torment of cancer eating away at the life-giving cells of the human body. We are, however, more likely to be obsessed than possessed by the demons who invade our night voyages and disrupt sleep.

The most famous demons that invade sleep are the incubus and succubus, nocturnal seducers of women and men that take over temporary possession in order to experience the delights of sexual activity. This is not only popular credulity, but theologians attribute a considerable role to incubi and succubi. Paracelsus (1493?–1541), who was both a doctor and a great thinker, was one of the first to consider succubi and incubi imaginary visions and not real people or even discarnate spirits. His definition relates today to the findings of modern psychoanalysts, who catalogue succubi and incubi as sexual fantasia. Like those suffering pain who are told is is psychosomatic, those who feel they are receiving the attentions of incubi or succubi go through tremendous distress and feel that they are, indeed, temporarily possessed.

I once had a client who confided in me that she had a demon lover who visited her nearly every night. She felt that she was being raped psychically and lived in fear of becoming pregnant and giving birth to a child of the devil. She was married and seemed to have a good relationship with her husband and family and in every other way was a pleasant, rational woman. Well, she became pregnant and had an abortion, feeling that at least she could defeat the devil in that way. This happened about twenty years ago in England; at that time few people were as permissive toward abortion as they are today, so it was a tremendous decision for her to make. She was, and still is, a good mother and loved

97

her children. After the abortion the visits from her demon lover never occurred again, to the relief of both of us.

We are not very far away from the Middle Ages when we come into contact with cases of possession. In those days every witch was thought to have sexual relations with the devil, and many innocent women were hanged or burned alive. Nothing more was needed than a casual reference to a horrible nightmare for this to happen. Even women who gave birth to children in the Middle Ages were suspected of having sexual commerce with the devil, and unfortunate children born with clubfeet or noticeable birthmarks were considered to be spawn of the devil.

You think this does not happen today? I can assure you it does. True, it is modified, but how many can honestly say that they do not recoil from malformed people with more than the usual amount of repulsion and distaste. In the Middle Ages hunchbacks could always find a home under the patronage of members of the upper classes—not because the upper classes were charitable but because they believed the hunchback was an offspring of the devil. They hoped the devil might in time consider their looking after the misformed people a gracious act and leave them alone. The hunchback was the patron's insurance against demonic activity in his own life.

When I was a child in the south of France, I loved to wander around the gardens of the famous casino of Monte Carlo. I remember a hunchback man who told me he earned a living simply by standing near the entrance to the Casino. No gambler ever entered without touching his back "for luck" and rewarding him with money for the privilege. The hunchback was still there when I was a teen-ager, and nothing had changed. I asked him why people touched the hump on his back, for I was no longer satisfied with the "good luck" theory. I discovered the little hunchback was something of a philosopher. "Most of the people who go there," he said, nodding toward the casino, "are already on the path to damnation. They know it, too. When they finally get to hell, I suppose they think it will help them to say they are at least on nodding terms with one of the devil's demons. That's me, of course." He said all this without bitterness.

Temporary possession during nightmares has given us a legacy of innumerable works of art and poetry. Study the work of the great Spanish painter Goya, especially the magnificent series called the "Caprices," or read about the impressive succubus in the *Contes Drolatiques* of Honoré de Balzac. Even the Arthurian legends are not untouched by demonic possession. The wizard Merlin was regarded as the issue of a liaison between a beautiful maiden and an incubus. Nearer our own times we find that in country areas of Germany, people born looking like animals are considered the offspring of a demonic rape. Right up to the Second World War, I remember that in certain sections of the world the Germans were frequently referred to as "the Huns." Behind the history of the Huns there is an entire system of legend referring to their gross, bestial and barbaric nature, with the explanation that the Huns were born of women who consorted with the devil or any of his legion of demons.

So long as we have evil touching life, so we shall always have the devil in one of his many disguises, taking over certain individuals as hostages by possession of the body, mind and spirit.

Chapter Seven

With Authority and Power He Commandeth*

When Father Michael V. Gannon was interviewed by the *Sentinel Star*, of Orlando, Florida, he was asked how many exorcisms have been conducted in the U.S.A. Presumably the interviewer was interested in exorcisms that occurred during the twentieth century. Father Gannon, assistant professor in the department of religion at the University of Florida and director of the Spanish mission Hombre de Dios, in St. Augustine, replied that only three exorcisms had taken place. Most parapsychologists would argue this point with Father Gannon. The fact that only three may have been recorded by the Roman Catholic Church does not mean that many more have not taken place. The priest quoted three classic cases: The first was the exorcism of a forty-year-old woman in Earling, Iowa, who was possessed from 1902 to 1928. The second was the case of the fourteen-year-old boy in Maryland who became the source for the film, *The Exorcist*. The third and most recent case occurred in the summer of 1973, in San Francisco.

*Luke IV:36

In my research I have talked with literally hundreds of people all over the world who have performed exorcisms; they include Roman Catholic priests, mediums and parapsychologists, plus a goodly number of witch doctors. Members of orthodox churches are remarkably reluctant to admit they have been called in to perform exorcism, and discussion was generally very difficult. On the other hand, from Hawaii to Africa there was no restraint in our conversation, and I was impressed by the completely open and down-to-earth approach everyone but Roman Catholic priests have toward the subject. The three cases most discussed in this country are, indeed, those mentioned by Father Gannon—chiefly because they were well documented, not only in theological circles but also by the press.

In 1928 a woman now known as Miss S. left her hometown in Michigan and moved to Earling, Iowa. She had shown signs of being possessed, refused to take communion or pray, and would never pronounce the name of Christ. Her family went through every phase of obtaining medical help for her, but she suffered from no known disease; neither was there any sign of mental illness. Finally her family appealed for help to the Catholic Archdiocese of Des Moines. They specifically asked for an exorcism—and that Father Theophilus Riesinger, a Capuchin monk, should perform this religious duty. Permission was granted to perform the exorcism, and in September of 1928 Miss S. was taken to a bedroom at the Sisters of St. Francis Convent in Earling, Iowa. Father Riesinger came in from Marathon, Wisconsin.

When he appeared in the bedroom, Miss S. fought so strongly against him that several nuns attempted to restrain her. As he commanded the demons to leave her, she freed herself from the nuns, leaped from the bed and soared through the air. After many attempts, she was pulled down from the air and the exorcism continued.

Father Riesinger quite properly demanded that the demons identify themselves, and they said they were Judas, Beelzebub, and also the father of Miss S., who said he was damned to eternity for a horrible sin. Also present was Mina, the father's girlfriend, who said she had murdered four children. These devils frequently tore down the pyx, the container holding the Blessed Sacrament.

Miss S. uttered obscenities in German, Latin and English. Whenever Father Riesinger moved near to her with any sacred relic, the woman howled like an animal, the sounds turning to screams of pain as she begged him to go away and remove the relics. As holy water was sprinkled on her, she screamed that it was burning her.

The rites continued for twenty-three days, and the convent was filled with eerie noises. All the forces of the Lord and his angels were called upon during the exorcism, as the priest persisted in his attempts to dislodge the demons within her. Miss S. began to refuse food and water and seemed to be dying. And, as the exorcism continued, it was feared that she would, indeed, die. On the twenty-third day her stomach became so swollen that the increased weight caused the bed to sag, but the battle was over for the possessed and the exorcist. Miss S. sat up in bed and said, "Praised be Jesus Christ. My Jesus is merciful."

While things were bad enough in the actual room of the exorcism, all was not well in the convent and in one of the churches associated with it. In 1928 the Reverend Arthur Ring served in St. Joseph's, and the exorcism was the subject of a conversation he had with the Reverend Joseph Steiger, pastor of the church where the rites were taking place. The Reverend Ring, now pastor of St. Paul's, recalls:

> Father Steiger went to deliver communion at a nearby farm. He was returning when a black curtain suddenly descended in front of him. He crashed his new car into a bridge, totally wrecking it. At the same time as this happened, one of the demons told Father Reisinger, "Well, I fixed your partner."
>
> On another occasion during the exorcism, Father Steiger awoke to hear what he thought must be rats running around in the walls of his room. He put on his stole, blessed the room, and the rats vanished.

Neighbors near the convent reported that the howls of rage from Miss S. could be heard for several miles. But now everything is serene in the convent. Nuns still sleep in the bedroom where the exorcism was held, and none has suffered any discomfort. With the official consent, the imprimatur, of Bishop Joseph F. Busch, the Reverend Carl Vogel published a pamphlet called *Begone Satan*. As with all official Roman Catholic reports, once an exorcism has been completed, there is rarely any follow-up of news of the formerly possessed. Many attempts have been made to seek out Miss S. But few such victims in the Western world will talk about the experience, perhaps because some of the memory is mercifully obliterated. But in the interest of full research, it bends the imagination to know how the possessed are able to take up the threads of life again.

The next "official" case (in terms of Roman Catholic

involvement in the United States) took place in 1949, when a fourteen-year-old boy living in Mount Rainier, Maryland, was possessed. (It is this case on which William Blatty based his best-selling novel.) The supernatural powers began to show themselves on January 15, 1949, when the boy, Jim X., was at the home of his grandmother. The sound of running water and of animals scratching came from beneath the floorboards in the grandmother's room and continued for several nights. The boy's father called in a pest exterminator to destroy what he believed to be rats. But no sign of any of these pests was discovered by the exterminator, and the eerie noises continued for ten more days.

Jim X. slept on the first floor of the house, and one night the shoes under his bed began to move and make scratching noises. The boy's mother and grandmother heard footsteps coming toward them, and accompanying the sound of the footsteps was the heavy beat of a drum.

Naturally the family was glad of any excuse to get out of the house, but it seemed that no matter where they went, strange phenomena caught up with them. One day, while riding with his aunt, mother and father, a rug on the back seat began to curl up, and an invisible force seemed to hold the mother and Jim X. in their seats. They were, naturally enough, terrified, and succeeding events did nothing to ease the tension. As they arrived at their destination, the home of the boy's aunt, Mr. X. was surprised to find that the ignition key to the car was not in the switch. He found it under the front seat, but no one knew how it had gotten there. The family was fearful and confused, but it was only when the boy's aunt died some days later that they began to think that some supernatural force was literally out to get one of them.

By that time Jim X. was finding it hard to get any sleep because of disturbances. It was bad enough when there were snarling noises and what appeared to be pests roaming around the woodwork, but now the force behind the noises was actually attacking him in his bed. Waves of cold swept through the room and were felt by his mother and grandmother. Sometimes they were knocked over as they tried to enter the room where the boy lay writhing on his bed. Food was flung around in the kitchen, and plates fell off tables. At school Jim X.'s desk suddenly shot across the floor, toppling over everything that got in its way.

By now the family was convinced that whatever was causing the disturbance was evil enough to warrant the utmost concern. They took Jim X. to spend the night with a Lutheran minister, but the manifestations continued even in the minister's house. He was thrown from his bed and the minister arranged a temporary mattress for him on the floor in his room, but the writhings of the mattress persisted.

It was just six weeks after the first scratching noises were heard that ugly red marks appeared on Jim X.'s skin. They are described as being like brand marks, and some lettering was clearly distinguished. Mr. and Mrs. X. were resolved to take their son to St. Louis, Missouri, to receive medical attention. There, neither physicians nor psychiatrists could discover anything wrong with Jim. By now the family was beginning to think the boy was possessed, and although of the Lutheran faith, they decided to consult a local Roman Catholic priest. He advised them to recite special prayers, gave them holy water to sprinkle around the house, and presented them with candles he had blessed.

Heartened by the fact they could be involved in some practical means to prevent the phenomena from recurring, they returned home with the firm intention of ending the disturbances. This was not to be the case, for when prayers were said, the phenomena increased. The bottle of holy water flew across the room but was unbroken. The bed became agitated when Mrs. X. sat down and lit the candles.

Frequent visits to St. Louis were made, but the manifestations increased and were witnessed by four uncles, two aunts and four cousins. On March 7, 1949, Mrs. X. decided to hold a séance with one of her sisters using a primitive method of the Ouija board. Other members of the family were present, and through asking questions they learned it was the spirit of the deceased aunt that inhabited the body of young Jim X. A Jesuit priest stationed in St. Louis was invited to witness the séance, and he prayed that the troubled spirit of the aunt would find rest. This proved to be useless, and again aggravated the situation. More manifestations followed.

The Jesuit priest returned with Father Bowdern, and both priests recited prayers over Jim. They also blessed him with a relic of St. Francis Xavier, and left two crucifixes under the pillow of the tired boy. The two priests prepared to leave the house, believing they had helped decrease the phenomena. As they left the room, the heavy bookcase in the bedroom swung around, a crucifix flew from the pillow around the room while a second crucifix moved toward the foot of the bed and a heavy bench overturned. The bed rocked all the time, and anguished relations called on the spirit of the deceased aunt to stop its activities.

On March 16, 1949, the Archbishop of St. Louis granted Father Bowdern permission to perform an exorcism, using the formal rites of the church. At least there was, in this case, more speed in granting permission than had been accorded to poor Miss S. of Earling, who was possessed for more than ten years, but the danger was not yet over. On the night of March 16, Father Bowdern was accompanied to the house of Mr. and Mrs. X. by a Jesuit scholar who was to assist him. They led Jim X. in an Act of Contrition and proceeded with the formal ritual of exorcism, commencing with a firm demand for the demon to reveal its name. This was followed by questions asking when the demon was prepared to leave the boy in peace.

Almost immediately Jim X. went into contortions, crying out with pain. The two priests continued their work, but the body of Jim X. was branded thirty times. Livid red marks scrawled themselves over his chest, throat, stomach, back and legs, rupturing his skin savagely and causing blood to flow. At one point the word HELL appeared in two-inch-high letters on the boy's chest, and then the horrifying portrait of a demon showed itself. The priests continued to perform the entire rite of exorcism every day for a week. It must have been a grueling experience for them, since the ritual takes at least forty-five minutes. The dedicated priests sometimes had to go through the ritual several times each night, interrupted by the boy's attacks on them.

The boy in turn was seen to be suffering as no human

being could ever be expected to suffer and survive. Each attack made him weaker and weaker while the forces of the demon grew stronger. He spoke in foreign languages, just as Miss S. had done, and the most profane obscenities flowed from the mouth of the young boy. The room continued to smell foul and this was accentuated by the frequent urinations and the expelling of foul matter from the victim.

Nothing seemed to alleviate the situation, which was rapidly deteriorating. On March 21, 1949, the priests persuaded the parents to transfer Jim X. to a hospital in St. Louis and then to a local rectory.

There the parents gave permission for Jim X. to become a Catholic. It was explained to them that the sacrament of holy communion is believed to be one of the most effective antidotes to demonic possession. I disagree with this, since one of the most terrifying exorcisms I ever conducted myself was to a Roman Catholic priest who had been exposed to holy communion all his life. But in moments of dire distress human beings will clutch at straws.

Jim X. received several hours of religious instruction designed for his conversion to Catholicism. But soon the phenomena started again—more obscenities, more defecation, more shouting in foreign languages, and more wounds appearing on his body, which was rapidly becoming emaciated. Worse still, his attention was directed to the priests, on whom he spat, urinated and directed some shocking obscenities. Then the boy fell into a better sleep than he had experienced for several weeks; the sleep continued for a few days, although he is said to have had nightmares.

The disturbances stopped on March 26, and all was

quiet for five days and nights. Then Father Bowdern saw an X branded on the boy's chest, and interpreted it to mean that the possession would stop after ten more days. On March 31, Jim X. again showed signs of being violently possessed, and life was a replica of the preceding days. Obscenities, urination, foul language and more red marks on the body. The rites of exorcism began again with the demon responding and insulting the priests. John was then baptized in the Roman Catholic faith and given his first holy communion before returning to the home of his parents, accompanied by the faithful Father Bowdern.

Within a few days they were back in St. Louis again. The demon firmly stated he was always with Jim and proved it by more manifestations of control over the boy's mind and body. As April progressed, there seemed to be no end to the constant exorcism ritual; it seemed as if it would go on forever. Then one day Father Bowdern read about an exorcism that had taken place in 1870 in Wisconsin.

On April 18, Bowdern forcibly made the boy wear a chain of religious medals around his neck and with some difficulty forced a crucifix into his hands. Then he continued with the ritual. The boy seemed to be interested in the Latin prayers, often stopping the priest and asking him to explain them. At this stage Father Bowdern felt it necessary and prudent to ask the demon if he would leave the body of the poor boy.

No sooner had he asked the question than all hell seemed to let loose. Jim seemed to have extraordinary strength as he lurched around, attacking the priest. It took the strength of four brothers to restrain him. At eleven P.M. the priests, still holding the boy down, were

110

also praying. In the name of Saint Michael, Father Bowdern commanded the demon to leave the boy's body. Again the body of the tormented child lurched and struggled in the most violent spasms he had ever experienced. Still Father Bowdern continued, and gradually the spasms subsided and Jim said in a quiet, almost normal, voice: "He is gone."

He talked to the priests, smiled at them and said that he felt very well. Twelve days later he returned home to his parents in Mount Rainier, Maryland.

At least we have a little postexorcism news of Jim. He is now thirty-eight years old, married and has three children. He has no recollection of the three months during which a demon held possession of him, and it is hoped that no one will try to probe the recesses of his memory to remind him of it. It is conceivable that he may have been one of the millions of people who have seen the movie, *The Exorcist*, and one can only wonder what effect, if any, it had on him. I worry about this. Some long-forgotten memory is surely stored in his subconscious, and one of the dangers of this film is that some people who have been possessed may see it and feel the old horror of possession returning. I am convinced the devil does not give up easily on his victims, and this is proved by the difficulties of exorcism. If people suffering from amnesia can be jolted back into full realization of things past, then it is feasible to think that the impact of something like this startling film could conceivably produce the same result.

One of the first recorded incidents of exorcism after the release of *The Exorcist* occurred in San Francisco. It started in May of 1972, and the case is interesting because it involved the possession of an entire family:

111

mother, father and a two-year-old son. Mr. B. was an immigrant Jew born in Britain who came to San Francisco in 1961. His wife was a Catholic and I presume that the child was baptized in the faith of his mother.

The home of Mr. and Mrs. B. started to become disturbed on May 27, 1972, when household items were thrown around the rooms by nonphysical forces. Black clouds were seen moving from room to room, and the phenomena were not confined to one room at a time. It was not unusual for knives from the kitchen to come whirling through the air at the same time as dishes were thrown on the floor in the living room and shoes in the bedroom gyrated macabrely. The family sought help from their local clergymen, and following a period of prayers, the bizarre happenings ceased.

But the house could never be the same again for the B. family, and they moved to another residence and yet another. On the anniversary of the first psychic upheaval, May 27, 1973, the entities returned to renew their activity and disrupt the comfort of the family. This time the eerie happenings were not confined to attacks on inanimate objects; the entities returned to renew their activity and disrupt the comfort of the family. This time the eerie happenings were not confined to attacks on inanimate objects; the couple was attacked. Something attempted to strangle them, and they were beaten and hit by objects flying through the air. Everything they loved and cherished in personal possessions was smashed, and small fires frequently appeared in the house. More than twenty people outside the family witnessed various aspects of the destruction, and in June of 1973, Mr. and Mrs. B. sought help from their parish priest. He refused to help them for reasons known only to himself, and the family continued to live in despair until a nun put them in touch with the Reverend Karl Patzeit. He visited the house to decide if an exorcism was necessary and personally witnessed several abnormal incidents.

Mrs. B. was thrown onto the floor by unseen hands, and her wedding ring wrenched from her finger; a paper bag in the kitchen burst into flames; and the two-year-old child began to scream in his bed. On investigation, part of the bed was found to have been destroyed and fragments of it were inside the bed. This is the first official record of the child being directly involved.

Father Patzeit is a Byzantine Jesuit and head of the Russian Catholic Church of San Francisco. He is a serious-visaged, aesthetic-looking man with enough presence of mind to take a photograph of some of the phenomena, such as the now well-known photo of a huge bite taken out of a sandwich. With the evidence of personal observation and consideration that the spiritual welfare of the family was at stake, Father Patzeit approached his archbishop on August 1, 1973, with a request that the case should be considered one of legitimate possession.

As soon as he did this, the demonic activities against the family were increased. There were further attacks on the persons of Mr. and Mrs. B., as well as the now everyday incidents of destruction of property. On August 16, 1973, the archbishop gave his permission for the sacred rites of exorcism to take place. The priest was given relics of the Holy Cross, the cross on which Jesus Christ is believed to have died, and two versions of the exorcism rites, one written in Latin, the other in English.

Father Patzeit returned to the unhappy household and began the exorcism. There was no immediate alleviation of the incidents, and it is now common knowledge that when exorcism first begins, the demons react to it with greater violence. That is why it is most important that any priest (or, indeed, anyone else involved in exorcism) be totally sure of his own religious affiliation and be tremendously dedicated to the efficiency of the rites. He must be irrevocably convinced that he will prevail through the influence of God and all the saints. Human failings and error on the part of a person performing an exorcism can be fatal to the results; it was the flaw in the young priest in *The Exorcist* which resulted in the death of the older priest. The spiritual aspects and convictions of the exorcist must be of the highest caliber, for most devils thrive on the weaknesses of mankind.

After thirteen unsuccessful attempts at exorcism, Father Patzeit was able to release the family from the demons on September 18, 1973.

The case of Mr. and Mrs. B. is different from those of Miss S. and Jim X., and I am inclined to think that the family suffered from poltergeist activity rather than true possession. They were the victims of attack, which is usual in the activities of mischievous ghosts, but there is no evidence that the personality of either Mr. or Mrs. B. was transformed, as it would have been if a demon had actually invaded the body. It was correct to apply the rite of exorcism, but probably for the wrong reasons, and many members of other churches have been quick to take up this point. A controversy still exists over the validity of the alleged possession. That help was needed is perfectly clear; but whether it was possession by demons of the bodies of Mr. and Mrs. B. will be a conversation point for many years.

To me the end product—a family relieved from the pressure of uneasy spirit and gaining peace of mind and body—more than justifies the action taken by Father Patzeit. On the other hand, with Professor Hans Holzer I must have been involved in more than five hundred similar cases where discarnate spirits have played havoc with families. But I have also performed several hundred exorcisms of a different kind, running parallel to the cases of Miss S. and Jim X. To my mind there is a vast difference in beholding a human body reduced to animal qualities, and knowing that this same human being can continue to suffer if help is not given.

Frankly, I believe from my own experience that dramatic incidents of poltergeist activity are tame stuff compared with the horrors of truly personal possession. I must emphasize, however, that Father Patzeit did a good job at the right time, but for the wrong reasons. Part of the duty of the clergy and priests is to bring comfort to those who need it, and he certainly did this. If there was an element of overkill in quelling the unruly spirits haunting the house of Mr. and Mrs. B., it was justified, and nothing can detract from the courage shown by Father Patzeit and his dedication to duty in helping the unfortunate people suffering in the Daly City household. He can never be accused of the sin of not caring for the plight of others, and the end product of peace in the household is proof enough of the efficacy of exorcism.

For once, the orthodox church rose to meet the needs

of its followers, and the only mistake seems to be that the first application for exorcism was turned down, adding months of misery for the family. For too many years parapsychologists have been forced to perform duties the clergy could and should perform. I can testify that there is never any shortage of miserable people, tormented with strange psychic happenings within their households, and not enough parapsychologists to cope with them.

Since the release of *The Exorcist,* a great deal of responsibility is placed on the clergy and on parapsychologists. First, there is likely to be a rash of public hysteria. Horror of all kinds walks with us today, and the occult explosion has alerted people to the fact that discarnate spirits can affect life. But we also have to cope with the hunger of many people for the macabre and their own unlimited imagination. So assessment of the necessities of any case is increasingly important to any exorcist today. First he must decide if there is a genuine case of possession, or poltergeist activity, or other psychic phenomena. Witnesses become important in this assessment, as do the mentality and caliber of the individual seeking help.

Unfortunately there are flaws on the part of some parapsychologists working today, some of whom seek involvement in psychic activity in order to make headlines. Many genuine cases carefully resolved by priests and parapsychologists never receive publicity; however, most practitioners keep meticulous records, and these make more interesting reading than the hyped-up versions in newspapers. Not that I blame the newspapers for following through, because all occult happenings make good, salable stories that increase readership. I simply feel it is a mistake to produce oversensationalized versions, often inaccurately reported, simply in order to boost sales.

A family in distress through obsession or possession needs help and needs it quickly. Not too long ago a priest was the natural confidant concerning anything that abnormally affected family life, but this does not appear to be the case today. In every case that has come directly to me I have always suggested that the people concerned should first visit a clergyman. To a certain extent I suppose I do this to protect myself, since I belong to an ancient religion that is far removed from the orthodox structures of many churches. I am not an evangelist for my own religious feelings, and never seek to "convert" others. Far too many priests have little or no faith in the exorcism rites supplied by their own church and seem to want to live like laymen. If a priest accepts all the dogma of his church, then he should go all out and accept everything; otherwise we shall witness nothing more than a watered-down version of the major religions of the world. Most of the people who come to me say they are afraid to go to their priest or they have already been rejected. It is not unusual for a priest to ask for *scientific* evidence that a person is possessed by evil spirits. I find this ludicrous; certainly he should ask for evidence, but to add "scientific" to it is almost laughable—if it were not so sad.

When we get down to the bare bones of religion, there is no scientific evidence of anything, for the great religions of the world have been built on the intangible quality of faith—and belief in such faith. One thing Father Patzeit proved is that possession brings into focus the reality of the Devil, and if the Devil is real, then God must be. In this lies the hope of a more harmonious life for most of mankind—especially if we reduce the whole thing to the eternal combat of evil against good.

Those who have faith know that good must ultimately win over evil, and this is the foundation on which all religions are based—not on scientific evidence. Without that belief, man on this planet makes no sense and becomes less than all the other creatures on the earth. Given the attribute of reason, which places man above all the other creatures of the earth, some of this power has to be used to differentiate between good and evil. In the framework of religious structures this becomes God and the Devil, thus fulfilling one of the basic laws of the universe: that there is a polarity in everything.

Chapter Eight

Exorcism—the Waterloo of Devils

The expulsion of an evil spirit by ritual, prayer and command is called exorcism. At the root of exorcism there is the firm belief that a discarnate spirit can invade the body of a living being, function and perform mischief through the use of the body. Since all things in nature and the supernatural exist by the universal law of polarity, then it is appropriate that the possessed can become depossessed.

Exorcism as a profession has been with us since primitive times, and various forms of it are in evidence throughout the world. When we think of exorcism, it is naturally associated with the idea of evil spirits, but every Christian has been exorcised at least once in his lifetime. That is, if he has undergone the rites of baptism, for this is one of the most common forms of exorcism known in the world. In the folklore and fairy tales of all nations, the newborn child has always been considered a ripe target for the attentions of the devil. That is why many churches insist on baptism at a very early age. Babies who are born weak, or with any doubt of survival, are baptized within a few hours of birth if

119

the parents are devout in their religion. Baptism, of course, in Christian terms signifies the union of the child with Christ, hence, the word "christening," signifying the actual act of baptism in the name of the Son of God.

Christian baptism is of uncertain origin, although it is likely that Jesus and possibly his first disciples were baptized by John. But in the teachings and practice of Jesus, Himself, baptism was never made a condition of discipleship. It was after the death of Christ that baptism emerged as Christianity's distinctive initiatory rite. At first the rite seems to have been performed only in the name of Christ, but by the close of the first century, the Trinitarian formula had come into use as attested in Matthew XXVIII:19.

During the second century both the form and the significance of the baptismal rite were more specifically defined. The description by Justin Martyr (c. 100 A.D.) mentions that there should be a preliminary period of fasting when adults are baptized. The practice in North Africa in the time of Tertullian, who was born about 160 A.D., was much more formal. First came a period of fasting and confession. Then the candidate publicly denounced the devil. After that he professed acceptance of some doctrinal formula, and an invocation was pronounced over water to render it an effective sanctifying agency. The candidate was immersed three times in the name of each person in the Trinity. This was followed by the laying on of hands and the ritual closed with a ceremonial tasting of honey and milk.

The doctrine that infants will be saved in the life to come, whether baptized or not, was the view expressed by Protestants in reaction to the Augustinian view that unbaptized infants cannot be saved. The rite of baptism is regarded as extremely important among Roman Catholics. Viewed as a form of exorcism, it not only provides a tangible bond with God but also the recognition that a newborn child comes into the world tainted by original sin. The premise of this is that the evil that caused the fall of Adam and the expulsion from paradise is transmitted from generation to generation. Therefore, all descendants of Adam must be regarded as being of a perverted or depraved nature. Both characteristics are ideal ground for Satan to work upon and sow the seeds of temptation.

Exorcism comes from the Greek word *exorkismos*, meaning "to bind with an oath, to adjure." It especially implies the expulsion of evil spirits or demons from possessed persons or from objects and places. This expulsion is achieved by the utterance of an adjuration in which the aid of more powerful spirits or deities is invoked by name. A possessed person exorcized in this way is freed from evil caused by the presence of malevolent entities. Various formulas, singly and in combinations, with and without the invocation of the "name," came into use. Among these were entreaties, prayers, threats, commands, maledictions, quotations from sacred and magical writings.

Furthermore, through further extension of the meaning, exorcism implies any overt act or combination of acts, performed with or without a spoken formula, but specifically designed to expel demons. These include such techniques as flagellation, the application of various substances often magical in content, the production of loud noises and foul odors, and the offering of sacrifices, in addition to the signs or gestures

121

as well as the use of charms, phylacteries and amulets. It is safe to say that if the number of demons is legion, then so are the means of expelling them and thus obtaining relief and salvation. Exorcism is universally practiced in primitive religions by the medicine man, the shaman, and, in more sophisticated religions, the priest. Exorcism certainly has an important place in all the higher religions, including Christianity. In order to demonstrate the power of Jesus over Satan, the Synoptic Gospels depict Him as exorcising demons, but through His own supernatural authority rather than the invocation of the name of God or by His help. Christians in both early and later periods exorcised in the name of Jesus rather more frequently than in the name of God. The official practice of exorcism was introduced into the Christian church at an early date, and exorcists formed one of the minor orders of the church. Their reputation helped spread the new faith. In his *Apologia,* Justin Martyr wrote:

> For many of our Christian men exorcised numberless demoniacs throughout the whole world and in the city of Rome, in the name of Jesus Christ. They have healed and do help them, rendering the possessing devils helpless and driving them out of men who could not be cured by all the other exorcists or by those who used incantations or drugs.

Later, in the third century, Origen, the great Christian scholar and teacher, stressed the efficacy of the letters of the word "Jesus,"

> whose name has already been seen, in an unmistakable manner, to have expelled myriads of evil spirits from

the souls and bodies of men, so great was the power it exerted on those from whom the spirits were driven out.

In Rome in 251, Pope Cornelius retained a team of fifty-two men as exorcists and they worked in the fourteen divisions of Rome. The present Catholic practice of prebaptismal exorcism, together with the exorcism of demoniacs and objects such as oil, water and salt, originated in early times. Today the priest alone is permitted to exorcise. The power attributed to the "name" of Jesus survives in the customary conclusion in Christian prayers, in which His name is invoked.

As an aid to exorcists—so that they could decide whether a possessing entity was good or evil—Vincentius von Berg compiled a manual of exorcism called the *Enchiridium.* An evil spirit could be identified if it showed any of the following tendencies:

1. Fled at the sign of the cross, holy water, the name of Jesus Christ.
2. Said anything against the Catholic religion.
3. Excited the mind of the possessed to express pride or despair.
4. Refused to discuss the possession with a priest.
5. Appeared with a loathsome or dejected appearance, or leaving a stench, noise, frightfulness or injury.
6. Approached mildly, but afterward left behind grief, desolation, disturbance of soul and clouds of the mind.

Berg also gave a list of indications by which it could be ascertained if anyone were bewitched into possession.

1. The bewitched desire the worst food.

2. They are unable to retain their food, are irked by continual vomiting, and are unable to digest.

3. Others experience a heavy weight in the stomach, as if a sort of ball ascended from the stomach into the gullet, which they seem to vomit forth, yet nevertheless it returns to its original position.

4. Some feel a gnawing in the lower belly. Others feel either a rapid pulsation in the neck or pain in the kidneys. Others feel a continuous pain in the head or brain, beyond endurance, on account of which they seem oppressed, shattered, or pierced.

5. The bewitched have trouble with the heart, which feels as if torn by dogs, or eaten by serpents, or pierced by nails and needles, or constricted and stifled.

6. At other times all parts of the head swell up, so that throughout the body they feel such lassitude that they can scarcely move.

7. Some experience frequent and sudden pains, which they cannot describe, but they shriek aloud.

8. In others the body is weakened and reduced to a shadow on account of extraordinary emaciation, impotency of vigor, and extreme languor.

9. At other times their limbs feel whipped, torn, bound, or constricted, especially the heart and bones.

10. Some are accustomed to feel something like the coldest wind or a fiery flame run through their stomach, causing the most violent contractions in their entrails and intense and sudden swelling of the stomach.

11. Many bewitched are oppressed by a melancholy disposition. Some of them are so weakened that they do not wish either to speak or converse with people.

12. Those injured by witchcraft may have their eyes

constricted, and the whole body, especially the face, almost completely suffused by a yellow or ashen color.

13. When witchcraft has by chance befallen the sick, he is generally attacked by some serious trouble, seized with fear and terror; if he is a body, he immediately bewails himself, and his eyes change to a dark color, and other perceptible changes are observed. Wherefore the discreet exorcist takes care to disclose the recognized signs of this sort to the relatives and those present to avoid scandal.

14. It is especially significant if skilled physicians are not sure what the affliction is, and cannot form an opinion about it; or if the medications prescribed do not help but rather increase the sickness.

15. Sometimes the only indications of bewitching are considered circumstantial and inferential, as employing witchcraft for hatred, love, sterility, storm-raising, ligature, or [harm to] animals.

Naturally this list was eagerly consulted when anyone was suspected of witchcraft, especially in the Middle Ages. The act of possession was just another crime placed on the heads of those who practiced the old religion of Wicca. In many cases, however, one did not need to be a genuine member of a coven; a neighbor's suspicion was enough. Behind this was not only a desire to clean up the community, but also opportunity to gain the assets of anyone accused and convicted of witchcraft. All land and other possessions of anyone so convicted were taken by the church, which adequately recompensed the person denouncing the witch. It was a sure way to make some easy money on the side. In view of the thousands of persecutions promoted against witches, I wonder if the thought of money may have overridden the official desire to save souls.

Although it was forbidden to ask the possessed the name of the person who had caused the possession, there was always someone around who was eager to affirm that he had proof that he knew the name of the person causing the evil. However, as the result of the trial of Father Louis Gaufridi, when he was convicted of conferring with and being possessed by the devil, a law was passed in 1620, which stated that the testimony of devils should not be accepted in any court of law. The University of Sorbonne in Paris, France, judiciously and seriously stated that the devil could not be expected to tell the truth. The law was not carried out stringently, and there is evidence that some devils did have their day in court.

In the Middle Ages, when an individual case of possession did not justify a lengthy exorcism, or if there were any doubt, the priest was allowed to play safe by pronouncing a general exorcism.

> Fixing his eyes firmly on the possessed person, and laying his hand on his head, in this position, with a secret command to the devil, because the devil himself is the originator of evil, the exorcist makes a certain sign, urging the possessed man publicly:
>
> "I, N., minister of Christ and the Church, in the name of Jesus Christ, command you, unclean spirit, if you lie hid in the body of this man created by God, or if you vex him in any way, that immediately you give me some manifest sign of the certainty of your presence in possessing this man . . . which heretofore in my absence you have been able to accomplish in your accustomed manner."

More and more rules for exorcism were continually being added to the numerous ones already in existence and in 1626, Maximilian van Eynatten produced his 1,232-page *Thesaurus Exorcismorum*. An examination of this remarkable work shows that van Eynatten left nothing out. He covered every eventuality, each with an appropriate rite, ranging from a conjuration against the "antique serpent," noxious pests (including caterpillars and locusts), the evil spirits that wreck matrimony, and any demon causing vexation in a house.

The 1947 New York edition of the *Rituale Romanum* reproduced verbatim the text as written by Maximilian van Eynatten, together with an introduction by Francis Cardinal Spellman, a personal friend of the Kennedy family. The priest, robed in a surplice and a violet stole, places one end of the stole around the neck of the possessed person (bound if he is violent) and sprinkles those present with holy water. Then the service begins.

1. The Litany.
2. Psalm 54 ("Save me, O God, by thy name").
3. Adjuration imploring God's grace for the proposed exorcism against the "wicked dragon" and a caution to the possessing spirit to "tell me thy name, the day, and the hour of thy going out, by some sign."
4. The Gospel (John I; and/or Mark XVI; Luke X; Luke XI.)
5. Preparatory prayer. Then the priest, protecting himself and the possessed by the sign of the cross, placing part of his stole round the neck and placing his right hand on the head of the possessed, resolutely and with great faith shall say what follows:
6. First Exorcism:
"I exorcize thee, most vile spirit, the very embodi-

ment of our enemy, the entire specter, the whole legion, in the name of Jesus Christ, to ✠ get out and flee from this creature of God ✠.

"He himself commands thee, who has ordered those cast down from the heights of heaven to the depths of the earth. He commands Thee, He who commanded the sea, the winds, and the tempests.

"Hear therefore and fear, O Satan, enemy of the faith, foe to the human race, producer of death, thief of life, destroyer of justice, root of evils, kindler of vices, seducer of men, betrayer of nations, inciter of envy, origin of avarice, cause of discord, procurer of sorrows. Why dost thou stand and resist, when thou knowest that Christ the Lord will destroy thy strength? Fear Him who was immolated in Isaac, sold in Joseph, slain in the lamb, crucified in man, and then was triumphant over hell.

(The following signs of the cross should be made on the forehead of the possessed.) "Depart therefore in the name of the ✠ Father, and of the ✠ Son, and of the Holy Ghost; give place to the Holy Ghost, by the sign of the Cross of Jesus Christ our Lord, who with the Father and the same Holy Ghost liveth and reigneth one God, for ever and ever, world without end."

7. Prayer for success, and making the signs of the cross over the demoniac.

8. Second Exorcism:

"I adjure thee, thou old serpent, by the judge of the quick and the dead, by thy maker and the maker of the world, by him who has power to send thee to hell, that thou depart quickly from this servant of God, N., who returns to the bosom of the Church, with fear and the affliction of thy terror. I adjure thee again (✠ *on his forehead*), not in my infirmity, but by the virtue of the Holy Ghost, that thou depart from this servant of God, N., whom Almighty God hath made in his own image.

"Yield therefore; yield not to me, but to the minister of Christ. For His power urges thee, who subjugated thee to His cross. Tremble at His arm, who led the souls to light after the lamentations of hell had been subdued. May the body of man be a terror to thee (✠ *on his chest*), let the image of God be terrible to thee (✠ *on his forehead*). Resist not, neither delay to flee from this man, since it has pleased Christ to dwell in this body. And, although thou knowest me to be none the less a sinner, do not think me contemptible.

"For it is God who commands thee ✠ .

"The majesty of Christ commands thee ✠ .

"God the Father commands thee ✠ .

"God the Son commands thee ✠ .

"God the Holy Ghost commands thee ✠ .

"The sacred cross commands thee ✠ .

"The faith of the holy apostles Peter and Paul and of all other saints commands thee ✠ .

"The blood of the martyrs commands thee ✠ .

"The constancy of the confessors commands thee ✠ .

"The devout intercession of all saints commands thee ✠ .

"The virtue of the mysteries of the Christian faith commands thee ✠ .

"Go out, therefore, thou transgressor. Go out, thou seducer, full of all deceit and guile, enemy of virtue, persecutor of innocence. O most dire one, give place; give place, thou most impious; give place to Christ, in whom thou hast found nothing of thy works, who hath despoiled thee, who hath destroyed thy kingdom, who

129

hath led thee captive and hath plundered thy goods who hath cast thee into outer darkness, where for thee and thy ministers is prepared annihilation.

"But why, truculent one, dost thou withstand? Why, rash creature, dost thou refuse?

"Thou art accused by Almighty God, whose statutes thou hast transgressed.

"Thou art accused by his Son, Jesus Christ, our Lord, whom thou didst dare to tempt and presume to crucify.

"Thou art accused by the human race, to whom by thy persuasion thou hast given to drink the poison of death.

"Therefore I adjure thee, most wicked dragon *(draco nequissime)* in the name of the ✠ immaculate lamb, who trod upon the asp and basilisk, who trampled the lion and dragon, to depart from this man (✠ *let the sign be made on his forehead*), to depart from the Church of God (✠ *let the sign be made on those standing by*). Tremble and flee at the invocation of the name of that Lord at whom hell trembles, to whom the virtues of heaven, the powers and dominions are subject, whom cherubim and seraphim with unwearied voices praise, saying, Holy, Holy, Holy Lord God of Saboath.

"The word made flesh ✠ commands thee.

"He who was born of the Virgin ✠ commands thee.

"Jesus of Nazareth commands thee, who, although thou didst despise His disciples, bade thee go, crushed and prostrate, out of the man, and in His presence, when He had separated thee from the man, thou didst not presume to go into a herd of swine.

"Therefore, adjured now in his ✠ name, depart from this man, whom he has created. It is hard for thee to wish to resist. It is hard for thee to kick against the pricks ✠ . Because the more slowly thou go out, the more the punishment against thee increases, since thou despisest not men but Him who is Lord of the quick and dead, who shall come to judge the quick and the dead and the world by fire."

9. Prayer.

10. Third and final Exorcism:

"Therefore, I adjure thee, most vile spirit, the entire specter, the very embodiment of Satan, in the name of Jesus Christ ✠ of Nazareth, who, after His baptism in Jordan, was led into the wilderness, and overcame thee in thine own habitations, that thou stop assaulting Him whom He hath formed from the dust of the earth to the honor of His glory, and that thou tremble not at the human weakness in miserable man but at the image of Almighty God.

"Therefore, yield to God, who by his servant Moses drowned thee and thy malice in Pharoah and in his army in the abyss.

"Yield to God, who made thee flee when expelled from King Saul with spiritual songs through his most faithful servant, David.

"Yield to God ✠ who condemned thee in Judas Iscariot the traitor. For he beats thee with divine ✠ scourges, in whose sight, trembling and crying out with thy legions, thou hast said: What art Thou to us, O Jesus, Son of the most high God? Art thou come hither to torture us before our time? He presses on thee with perpetual flames, who shall say at the end of time to the wicked: Depart from me, ye cursed, into everlasting fire, which is prepared for the devil and his angels.

"For thee, impious one, and for thy angels are prepared worms which never die.

131

"For thee and thy angels is prepared the unquench-
able fire; because thou art the chief of accursed murder,
thou art the author of incest, the head of sacrilege, the
master of the worst actions, the teacher of heretics, the
inventor of all obscenities. Therefore, O impious one,
go out. Go out, thou scoundrel, go out with all thy
deceits, because God has willed that man be his temple.

"But why dost thou delay longer here?

"Give honor to God, the Father Almighty, to whom
every knee is bent.

"Give place to the Lord Jesus Christ ✠ who shed for
man His most precious blood.

"Give place to the Holy Ghost, who through his
blessed apostle Peter manifestly struck thee in Simon
Magus, who condemned thy deceit in Ananias and
Sapphira, who smote thee in Herod the King because
he did not give God honor, who through his apostle
Paul destroyed thee in the magician Elymas by the mist
of blindness, and through the same apostle by his word
of command bade thee come out of the pythoness.

"Now therefore depart. ✠ Depart, thou seducer. Thy
abode is the wilderness, thy habitation is the serpent. Be
humbled and prostrate. Now there is no time to delay.
For behold the Lord God approaches quickly, and his
fire will glow before him and precede him and burn up
his enemies on every side. For if thou hast deceived
man, thou canst not mock God.

"He expels thee, from whose eye nothing is secret.

"He expels thee to whose power all things are subject.

"He excludes thee, who hast prepared for thee and
thy angels everlasting hell; out of whose mouth the
sharp sword will go, he who shall come to judge the
quick and the dead and the world by fire."

The *Rituale Romanum* also had an appendix published in 1631. This one forms part of the ceremony for exorcizing a house troubled by an evil spirit. This short exorcism is generally pronounced by a priest, but many laymen today also use it.

Hearken, then Satan, I adjure thee, O serpent of old, by the Judge of the living and the dead, by the creator of the world who hath power to cast into hell, that thou depart forthwith from this house. He that commands thee, accursed demon, is He that commanded the winds and the sea and the storm. He that commands thee, is He that ordered thee to be hurled down from the height of heaven into the lower parts of the earth. He that commands thee is He that bade thee depart from Him. Hearken then Satan and fear. Get thee gone, vanquished and cowed, when thou art bidden in the name of our Lord Jesus Christ who will come to judge the living and the dead and all the world by fire. Amen.

The belief in possession and the acceptance of exorcism as the panacea is just as strong today as it was in the Middle Ages. In my own lifetime three subjects, once taboo as conversation pieces in everyday society— sex, death and possession—are now widely and freely discussed. From primitive countries to such huge cities as New York, London, Paris and Rome, more and more people are calling on exorcists for help. I admit that all such calls are not justified, but each case is worthy of consideration either by clergymen or dedicated people working in the field of psychic phenomena. If only one genuine case of possession is saved in any single year, then it is worthwhile sorting out the pseudo from the genuine. The Protestant church is just as concerned about exorcism as the Roman Catholic church, which prudently retained the rites of exorcism among its dogmas.

We can no longer state with certainty that every person feeling he is possessed must seek psychiatric help and be content with it. The exorcist is concerned with actually expelling external evil forces, while the psychiatrist is concerned with the state of mind and interaction on the emotions. Perhaps the simple answer to alleviating suffering is to break through the rigid bands of professional pride and so allow a merging of psychiatry and religious exorcism. It is not likely that this will occur yet, but within such a thought lies the hope of many in the future who will know the torments of being hostages of Satan and his legion of demons.

Unfortunately there is some confusion today between true possession and poltergeist activity. The two phenomena can go hand in hand. Many investigators of psychic phenomena have gained reputations for being able to cope with haunted houses and are to be commended for doing a good job in freeing spirits entrapped in these houses. But a haunting is not always a possession. As a medium, with Professor Hans Holzer and other parapsychologists, I have visited haunted houses but never confused this work with that of expelling evil spirits from possessed persons. The two types of phenomena can merge, but it is important to recognize the distinct difference. It will be a sad day when the majority of those who have experienced living in a haunted house suddenly begin to think they are possessed.

Gradually the furor created by the movie *The Exorcist* will die away, and the genuine exorcist will continue to go quietly about his business, never seeking to cash in on or sensationalize one of the most pathetic and acute miseries ever known to man. For as long as evil vies with good, we shall have people who are possessed; the exorcist will have plenty of work.

Chapter Nine

Shields Against the Devil

Exorcism by means of orthodox religious techniques always used the name of the deity and the trappings with which it is conversant. In the Christian religion we find the name of God, Jesus Christ, all the saints, and the sign of the cross essential parts of the rites of exorcism. The ability to free the possessed is not confined to members of the Christian faith, and each exorcist uses his specific belief to effect a cure. The witch doctor or shaman can be just as effective as the Christian priest.

From time to time, and particularly in the present century, numerous laws have been passed by governments that felt this age-old service had no place in efforts to uplift native society. But old traditions rarely die away, and exorcism still flourishes, even if done in secret. The main impact on most countries where exorcism is legally banned is that the witch doctor recognizes the greater hazards of his profession and so increases his fees. Shortly after World War II a law called the Suppression of Witchcraft was passed in South Africa, but it proved to be about as effective as a snowflake's survival in hell. True, from time to time practitioners have been fined and sentences imposed on some, but so long as possession, real or imagined, exists, there will be someone willing to perform exorcism. In 1967 all the leading London newspapers carried stories sent out on the wireservices to the rest of the world about South African witch doctors.

"The typical South African witch doctor serves as a psychiatrist, medical doctor, herbalist and exorcist," said the papers. "When herbal remedies fail, he uses psychology and if that fails, he utilizes the rites of exorcism as a means of relieving the patient's symptoms."

In Christian countries the Anglican church has been much more loquacious than the Roman Catholic church in accepting the fact that there has been a great surge of interest in Satanic cults. This is something no Western church has had to face officially for more than two hundred years, but priests of all denominations are now finding that it is part of their duty to cast out demons and exorcise the possessed. By recognizing an evil, there is more chance of relieving the cause of it—which is just about as logical as going for a regular checkup for cancer. By knowing the cause and effect, cures can be expected to be successful and to thoroughly appreciate good, one must sometimes face evil, if only on a comparative basis. Going hand in hand with the recognition of Satanic cults and the eternal fear and respect for the devil, comes an increasing business in the sale of amulets and talismans.

Man has always fashioned in his mind a host of invisible beings which became known as devils, demons and kindred evil spirits. He believes that these have the power to curse him and cause misfortune, but most of all that any one of them can possess him and endanger his soul. This fear of evil spirits has not diminished, and each generation seems to have become more devil-ridden than its predecessor. What once could have been dismissed as imagination has been reinforced by the major religions of the world as well as all the primitive ones. If man could expect help from his God, so he could also expect hindrance from the devil and his legion. But the main instinct in both the sophisticated and the primitive being is that of self-preservation and survival. So amulets and talismans were invented as a tangible defense against the intangible fear of the unknown or not understood.

The word "talisman" is found in many of the early Arabic languages, where it is translated "to make marks like a magician." But the Arabs borrowed it from the Greek word meaning "a consecrated religious object." An amulet is supposed to constantly exercise its powers on behalf of the individual, while a talisman is designed for one specific task. For instance, the St. Christopher medal, so popular with travelers, is a talisman designed to protect a person while traveling despite the fact that Christopher is now an impeached saint. Amulets gained respect as a permanent defense against evil because they are always inscribed with magical words or texts. From the amulet the charm came into being.

The Sumerians, Babylonians and Assyrians inscribed their spells on clay tablets and baked them. The Egyptians wrote them on sheets of papyrus, or on calcareous stone, potsherds, figurines of wood as well as on wax. Among the largest amulets are the stone stelae known as the Metternich stelae. The Jews wrote their amulets on parchment but in the Middle Ages used terra-cotta bowls and paper, while the Gnostics and Greeks, always noted for artistic talent, inscribed theirs on semiprecious stones. The Persians and Arabs carefully inscribed their spells on agate, onyx, and cornelian—also on the skin of unborn gazelles. From Japan we find amulets made of wood. The Chinese fashioned them with delicate brushwork on silk. Asian Indians produced amulets on copper plates, palm leaves and fine paper made from the bark of trees. Today we produce a multiple array of charms, amulets and talismans by means of the printing press, as well as all natural stones and man-made synthetic materials such as plastic. The reason and the method remain unchanged, although the materials available have increased. Such spells have always been thought to protect man from every known kind of devil and evil influence, and the great scientific age in which we find ourselves today is no exception.

Just as van Eynatten produced the most definitive book on exorcism, so Sir Hermann Gollanz produced his *Book of Protection,* published in London in 1912. Both have remained prime sources of reference for anyone interested in exorcism and the many tangible defenses against the devil.

Hundreds of years ago the Hebrews, ever conscious that evil spirits inhabit dwellings as well as human beings, produced terra-cotta bowls, which they buried under the four corners of the foundations of houses that once stood in the city now known as Hillah. The British Museum has a fine collection of these bowls obtained from archaeological expeditions between 1850 and 1960. The oldest bowl dates from the first century

B.C., and the most modern from the sixth century A.D. All have texts inscribed on them, designed to drive away the devil and the evil spirits Satan, Niriek, Zariah, Abtur Tura, Can and Lilith. These bowls were called devil traps. Some of the texts curse the devil. The lengthy period during which they were produced and consistently used shows an attempt to unite paganism, which permitted the use of devil traps, and the Hebrew religion, which forbade trafficking in magical ceremonies, spells and incantations.

The finger ring, popular in all ages, was not originally worn so much as a form of artistic decoration but rather as a protection from devils. Consistent with this is the worldwide use of circles of stones, relics of temples, for the circle itself was sacred and linked with the idea of life without end, infinity—no beginning and no end. The finger ring was, and is, a special kind of amulet and has always had a ceremonial value to indicate authority and protection. King Solomon had a magical ring; every pope has a ring. The nun taking her vows of chastity as a bride of Christ is guarded from evil influence by her ring; the everyday wedding ring was used for the same purpose. The Victorians produced mourning rings to protect a beloved deceased person from evil. Royal rings, coronation rings, papal rings, archepiscopal and episcopal rings, investiture rings, such as those worn by Masons, were all forerunners to the charm and zodiac rings in everyday use today. The purpose was always the same; the person wearing a ring, particularly one that has been blessed, can always hope that it will act as an amulet to ward off evil influences.

Of course the oldest amulet in the world is the cross, which is not only the major symbol of the Christian church but also one used by the people of western Asia and Europe long before the birth of Christ. The cross did not become the symbol of Christianity until the fourth century, although the custom of crossing oneself was common in the first century A.D. Crosses marked on houses as well as places of religious significance indicated the presence of god and as such became naturally repellent to Satan. When Satan, in the form of an Indian, came to attack him, Saint Anthony made the sign of the cross and frightened away the devil. When attacked by a demonic animal, he again made the sign of the cross and adjured the animal to depart in the name of God. The sign of the cross is still important in all exorcisms performed by priests and other clergy-men.

The crucifix is a variation on the cross and has the figure of Christ represented on it; with this double power, it is more efficacious in repelling devils than the simple cross. We can find examples of the crucifix on tombs in the first, second and third centuries A.D., but it did not become a public symbol or badge until the Emperor Constantine the Great caused it to be placed on the shield of his soldiers and removed the Roman eagle in the early fourth century A.D.

The ancient Christian Fathers said:

> The devils fear and tremble not only by reason of the Crucifixion of Christ but even at the sign of the cross wheresoever it be made apparent, whether it be depicted upon a garment or whether it be made in the air.

Gradually the cross began to be associated with magical powers as more and more people began to wear it, not

DRIVING OUT THE DEVILS

only as a symbol of faith but as a protective amulet. The pagan sorcerers conscious of its popular attributes of repelling evil forces also began to use it. This caused the Christian Fathers to complain that even laymen would drive away the devil simply by uttering the name of Christ and making the sign of the cross. Even exorcism has known professional jealousy.

One of the favorite forms of literature in the Middle Ages was based on the idea that men who desired power or wealth had the ability to make a contract with the devil. Such contracts are said to have been written on parchment with the blood of the man desiring union with the devil, who then carried it off to his subterranean archives. But the devil has always been known to be cunning, and he does not like to wait too long to get his pound of flesh, so all such contracts were for a specific number of years, during which the devil kept his part of the contract and gave the man his heart's desire. Then came the day of reckoning, and the interest on all the devil had given had to be paid in terms of the man's soul. The saints had a sporting chance to snatch the soul on its way to hell, but few legends have the devil give up his contract willingly.

The Ethiopian *Book of Saints*, circa 500 A.D., gives one of the earliest descriptions of the devil as a man instead of the early Panlike image complete with horns, cloven hooves and a tail. Here we find the devil described as a huge, dark man, with fiery eyes, ugly teeth, thin legs, long clawlike hands. His legion of lesser demons, however, have animal heads and tails, and all produce a sulfurous smell. In the usual form of contract the devil, either in his human or animal form, would say to his victim: "Dost thou believe in me, young man? Wilt thou deny thy Christ and not turn again to him when I have fulfilled thy desire?" The illusion of the devil in human form presumably made it all the more easy for the contract to be effected.

There is a story that Saint Basil effected the exorcism of a young man. The saint told him to pray for three days, but when Saint Basil came to him to inquire how things were going, the young man said he was still beset by the devil tormenting him. So Saint Basil prayed for him for forty days and nights, and the holy man rejoiced that he was gradually relieving the man from the temptations and the evil influence. Saint Basil was the Bishop of Caesarea, and as a final effort to save the man's soul, he called all his monks together and they all prayed. Then the man was brought to the church and all praised God and cried, "Lord, have mercy on us." Finally the parchment on which the man had denied Christ fell down from the roof of the church and was caught by the saint. Again the Lord was praised, the young man was blessed and the sacrament was given to him.

The Book of the Miracles of the Virgin Mary contains many stories of her intervention and power to rescue souls from Satan. In the richly illustrated book of her miracles we see her fighting valiantly against Satan for the souls of those in whom she was personally interested. She always won, but every soul had to repent before she could be sure of victory. Acceptance into the church almost always occurs after an exorcism, as we found in the three examples of the major exorcisms of the twentieth century; Miss S., Jim X. and the California couple all became members of the Roman Catholic Church.

Sir Donald Budge, the great Victorian authority on occultism and mysticism, relates the story of a man who fell foul of the devil and the deep sea. A young man in Antioch applied to Cyprianus, the Magician, for help in obtaining the love of the beautiful but virtuous Justina. When Satan went to get her, the maiden was always praying and the devil was defeated. Cyprianus felt that Satan was ineffectual—or trying to deceive him—and in a fit of pique burnt his books of magic. He then was baptized by the Archbishop of Antioch, became a monk, then a deacon, a full-fledged priest, and finally the Bishop of Carthage. He also made the virtuous Justina an abbess of a house of virgins. When Decius, the Roman Emperor (201–251), tried to force the bishop and Justina to worship idols, they refused to do so. The Emperor submitted them to torture and finally both the bishop and Justina were beheaded. To some this may seem as if the devil waited a long time for his revenge; torture and beheading seem a sad end for two dedicated servants of God.

The Inquisition or Holy Office of the Roman Catholic Tribunal was instituted by Pope Gregory IX in 1233, officially to suppress heresy. In 1320 the Inquisition was extended to deal with those who followed the ancient religion of Wicca, commonly called witchcraft, or were thought to do so. Established by King Ferdinand and Queen Isabella in 1479, with consent from the pope, the Spanish Inquisition was especially notorious. In this period we find persecution of a minority at its worst. Heresy was no longer the sole issue, and anyone thought to be in league with or possessed by the devil was brought to a crude form of trial where the victim was presumed guilty.

Saving souls from the devil was, however, a prime consideration, and the rites of exorcism were not

144

confined to the use of the Holy Name. The devil was expelled by brute force with tortures of the most dreadful nature. Under the influence of such ghastly man-made contraptions as the Iron Maiden and the rack and torture by pulling out fingernails and toenails, it is no wonder that nearly every victim confessed that he or she had had traffic with the devil or was possessed by him.

The victims were always given the chance to denounce the devil and his legion, and each confession was taken as a sign that torture had a place in exorcism since it seemed to prove effective. But even confessions did not save thousands of poor souls from death by fire. To leave anyone at liberty who was thought to have been possessed by the devil was not only a social crime but also a religious one. Demons were accepted as a public danger, and it is likely that Jesus recognized this when he transformed devils into swine.

During the Inquisition any form of execution could have been used as a punishment, but the final expulsion of the devil was usually achieved by fire, a reflection of the idea that fire is the greatest of all means of purification. Saint Jerome, in his commentary on the Prophet Nahum thought that death at the stake alone could help save those in league with the devil and free them from eternal damnation. A thousand years later his point of view was upheld by the Inquisition. It is likely that the inquisitors thought that God would not take vengeance twice upon the same subject and that those who have been punished once by fire would not later be subjected to the fires of hell. The end justified the means, and exorcism by torture was wrongly thought to be the swiftest way to save as many souls as

145

possible. While Roman Catholics were responsible for the terrors of the Inquisition, Anglican churches also took part to a lesser degree and on a smaller scale in the torture of victims accused of trafficking with the devil. In the light of Christian tactics to achieve exorcism by any means, the ancient magical rites of the pagans and others were much less intense and relied mainly on effecting the expulsion of the devil by the use of spells, incantations and the names of existing deities. The spell book of Nonarius III, sometimes called the Grimoire of Armadel, expresses a much more civilized means of driving out the devil.

> I adjure thee by the great and holy name of God that immediately and without delay, thou shalt appear before me in an agreeable form and without noise or hurt to my person and so to obey all that I shall command thee and I adjure thee in the name of the Living God and by these Holy Names: El Elohim, Elohom, Elophin, Sabaoth, Eieh, Adies, Adonay, Iah, Saday, Tetragrammaton, Sadyay, Agios, Theos, Ischiros, Athanatos Agla. Amen.

These names are a mixture of Hebrew and Greek but were deemed effective based on the belief that all exorcism relied on the principles of magic. The Inquisition demanded something much more dramatic despite the fact that in the ancient history of exorcism, there are numerous examples of tried-and-true formulas. But magic itself had become suspect and related to heresy since one of the attributes of witchcraft was the ability to use magic to perform what seemed to be miracles.

Chapter Ten

Attitudes of the Churches Toward Exorcism

Although the Jewish religion has a past history relating to spirit possessions and exorcism, it is difficult to get members of this faith to talk about their attitude toward exorcism today.

Ancient methods of exorcism consisted of coaxing out, insulting or terrorizing the demons. Coaxing implies a rather timorous attitude, inconsistent with the usual grandiose claims by exorcists of other religions. However, it was not uncommon in the time of Justin Martyr, who noted: "Now assuredly your exorcists make use of art when they exorcise, even as the heathens do, employing fumigations of incense and incantations." (*Dialogues with Trypho* LXXXV)

In the *Compendio dell Arte Essorcistica et possibilita della Mirabill*, published in Bologna MDXC, I found a "Benedidio incese ad profumigandum daemoniacos," which turned out to be a particularly noxious combination of smells—enough to scare any number of demons away. It consists of the following:

Galbani
Sulphuris
Affafoetida
Aristolochiae
Ypericonis
Rutae

The ancient book swears to its efficacy when burnt in the presence of a possessed person. Justin Martyr was probably aware of similar means of fumigation.

The case of Sarah, the daughter of Raguel, is one in which the system of disgusting the demon was brought into play. Raphael, the angelic friend of Tobias, advises that the heart and liver of a fish be laid on hot embers. The fumes from the putrid remains of the fish must have been outrageously irritating to the demon, since sulphuretted hydrogen and acrolein would be released. The fiend-splitting odor was sufficient to drive Asmodaeus posthaste to hell.

Flavius Josephus, the Jewish historian and writer, refers to the terrorizing of demons by Eleazar and witnessed by the Emperor Vespasian and members of his army. In this case the exorcist put an herbal, decorated ring to the nostrils of the possessed and drew the demon out through the nose. The possessed man fell down calling out the name of Solomon. The herb used was probably baaras, commonly known as mandrake, which is associated with strong magic. Baaras could be obtained only by yoking a dog to the root of the plant. As the dog pulled out the plant, he is said to have dropped dead. The main value of the plant depends on its association with demonic properties. Mandrake root resembles the figure of a man; it is said

148

to be possessed of supernatural qualities. Pliny refers to the Latin rite for gathering the plant and knew that it is also possessed of certain soporific and anaesthetic powers. The practice of Eleazar using mandrake clearly shows the relationship of Jewish demonology and exorcism to ethnic principles and customs. William Shakespeare refers to mandrake as "the insane root that takes the reason prisoner."

Eleazar used the mandrake with a ring, which has always played a part in the extraction of demons. Lucian in his *Philopseudes* mentions an iron ring obtained from a gibbet being used for a similar purpose. Spirits were supposed to enter the body via the mouth or nostrils, and the earring was originally a nose ring designed to guard the orifice. The earring has remained as an ornament, but the nose ring has disappeared in the West. Eleazar probably used a ring engraved with a "name," rendering it superpotent against all demons. By applying the mandrake and the ring to the nostrils of the possessed man, Eleazar had double insurance that the demon would depart.

There is also evidence in Jewish writings that water, light and loud noise were used in exorcisms. Certainly at early Jewish weddings a great deal of noise was generally made to frighten away evil spirits. Apparently today the old methods are swept under the carpet as if they never existed. Yet the driving away of evil spirits occurs in numerous Jewish rituals. The melancholia of Saul was attributed to an evil spirit, which was lured away by the sweet playing of the harp by David. In the Middle Ages, when the influence of the Cabala was at its height, exorcism was an integral part of Jewish life. The Cabala is the esoteric mystic lore of Judaism, based on an occult interpretation of the Bible and handed down as the secret doctrine of the initiated.

Even the ceremony of circumcision was, and is, considered an act of dedication of the body to the spirit in order to gain the protection of God. The sacrifice of the paschal lamb was to protect the Jewish inhabitants from "the destroying angel." The ceremonies remain and include the feasts (seders) of Passover, regarded as "nights of protection from demons."

There is no generic term for demons in the Jewish Bible, although the word *shedim* is used implying an "injurer." But rabbinical writings are filled with many references to the names, activities and characteristics of demons, as well as hints on how to expel and ward them off. The Talmud says that demons fly, can predict the future, they can assume human form and are capable of rotating their heads a full three hundred sixty degrees.

In Jewish folklore we find the Dybbuk, a spirit that enters a living body and never leaves until it is exorcised. If the guest spirit has inherited through reincarnation a massive load of guilt, it becomes a dybbuk, which is considered most harmful and therefore of necessity must be expelled by exorcism. In the sixteenth century any abnormal mental condition was attributed to the influence of a dybbuk. The Jewish laws of cleanliness and hygiene are well known, as is the idea that women are unclean because the devil will always try to possess a woman in preference to a man.

Imperfect woman seeks perfection with man, so the demons seek to unite themselves primarily with woman, who represents the next degree of creation above them. So women are more prone to sorcery than men; the sorceress is a woman through whom the devil that has possessed her operates, or one through close association with demons has acquired their malevolent attributes.

Joshua Trachtenberg,
Jewish Magic and Superstition

Carnal relationships between evil spirits and human beings have frequently been reported in Jewish literature, and the religion is noted for the fact that most orthodox Jews still use amulets designed to ward off the evil eye. Apparently the modern method of easing this horrible affliction is not by specific rites of exorcism but rather by general terms of advice. Man is considered capable of exorcising himself, which sounds very right and proper on paper, but I doubt if it is effective in cases of true possession. We know that reason and thought are the first things to flow away when a person is possessed. How, then, can he be adjured to "lead a straight, upright, moral life and read the scriptures"?

It goes without saying that members of any religion who faithfully believe and follow the dogmas of their specific religion stand a better chance of not being invaded by evil spirits. But this is asking a great deal of man, who is still in his imperfect state. But the attitude of the Islamic faith is very practical. Leaders of the church try to find out where a possessed person may have transgressed in his life. Again I feel it is difficult to believe it is possible to get straightforward answers when the devil or demons are in occupation. Explanations presumably must come from those who know the afflicted person, but secondhand knowledge may be tinged with personal imagination, as well.

151

Muslims have advisers and mentors, but no priest-hood. Magic and fortune-telling are unlawful to Muslims. Yet there is an entire structure of devils called the jinns and janns within the Koran, the sacred book of the Muslims. Generally the single name jinn is used, but not always in the context of being thoroughly evil or entirely good. Jinns can come in any shape or size, can crawl, walk or fly; some are in the form of men, while others are like animals or slither around like snakes. If the jinn is good looking or in a pleasing form, he is endowed with a good spirit; if he is horrible to look at, then he is evil. Certain jinns bring about destruction; others are said to have helped build the pyramids. Poetry and food are protected from jinns.

On the last night of the month of Ramadan, women sprinkle salt on the floor and call upon "the name of God, the Compassionate and Merciful."

Despite the modern leaders of Islam being reluctant to speak about exorcism, the *Jawahiru L. Khamsah* and *A Dictionary of Islam,* both published in 1885 by Dr. T. P. Hughes, refer to a combination of factors necessary for exorcism, and these include being aware that there is a harmonious connection of planets, elements and the number of times an incantation may be said. The exorcist is ordered to prepare himself by fasting for forty days in an isolated area. He is forbidden to converse with anyone and must abstain from a specific list of foods. The exorcist, himself, must, like Caesar's wife, be above reproach.

I find it most interesting that the Arabs, who were the early mathematicians and astrologers, should also take numbers and the planetary signs into consideration as part of an exorcism. During the long forty days of isolation and fasting, the exorcist is said to experience the highest joys of heaven and the horrors of hell. Muslims accept the existence of heaven and hell, so presumably there is a definite place for good and evil.

Most Muslims wear charms to combat the evil eye. The most popular charm is the hand of Fatima, representing the prophet, his daughter Fatima, Ali, her husband, and their two sons. The Islamic Center in London, England, is a stronghold of the faith, but its counselors seem to prefer to give spiritual comfort to the possessed while recommending a visit to a psychiatrist. Since no records of case histories are available, I can only hope that this method is effective. Otherwise, there is likely to be more work for the Roman Catholic exorcists. A demon expelled becomes a body and soul gained for the ever-increasing numbers of this church.

In considering the attitude of the Catholic church, we find a division between the Church of Rome and the liberal Catholics. In the Roman Catholic church exorcism is part of the duties of the priest but always under the jurisdiction of a higher authority, such as the bishop of the diocese to which the priest belongs. The Roman Catholic rite of exorcism is as impressive as all the other ceremonies for which this church is noted. The *Rituale Romanum* is the best-known rite of exorcism, although there are several shorter versions. Before an exorcism the designated priest is prepared by four prayers said over him by his bishop.

> Dearest children, who are about to be ordained to the office of Exorcist, ye must duly know what ye are about to undertake. For an Exorcist must cast out devils and announce to the people that those that may not be

present at the sacrifice must retire. And at the altar minister water to the priest. Ye receive also the power of placing your hand upon energumens and by the imposition of your hands and the Grace of the Holy Spirit and the words of exorcism, unclean spirits are driven from the bodies of those who are obsessed. Be careful, therefore, that as ye drive out devils from the bodies of others, so ye banish all uncleanness and evil from your own bodies lest you fall beneath the power of these spirits who by your ministry are conquered in others. Learn through your office to govern all imperfections lest the enemy may claim share in you and some dominion over you. For truly will ye rightly control those devils who attack others, when first ye have overcome their many crafts against yourselves. And this may the Lord vouchsafe to grant you through His Holy Spirit.

This first prayer is impressive and shows the seriousness with which the mission is endowed. The bishop then gives a copy of the rites of exorcism to the priest, saying: "Receive this and commit it to thy memory and have power to place thy hands upon energumens whether they be baptized or whether they be catechumens."

The third prayer is then said by the bishop:

Dearest brethren, let us humbly pray God the Father Almighty that He may vouchsafe to bless these His servants to the office of Exorcist, that they may have the power to command spirits, to cast forth from the bodies of those who are obsessed, demons with every kind of their wickedness and deceit. Through His only begotten Son, Jesus Christ, our Lord who with Him liveth and

reigneth in the unity of the Holy Spirit, one God, world
without end. Amen.

The potential exorcists continue to kneel for the final
prayer.

Holy Lord, Almighty Father, Eternal God, vouchsafe
to bless these thy servants to the office of Exorcists; that
by the imposition of our hands and the word of our
mouth, they may have power and authority to govern
and restrain all unclean spirits; that they may be skillful
physicians for Thy Church, that they may heal many
and be themselves strengthened with all Heavenly
Grace. Through our Lord Jesus Christ, thy Son who
with thee liveth and reigneth in the Unity of the Holy
Spirit, one God, world without end. Amen.

When the prayers are finished, the priest is first of all
made aware that he is going out on a special
project—that is, the casting out of devils. Any minor
fears are allayed by the assurance that his will to work
will be augmented by the help of the Holy Spirit. He is
warned that the best defense against demons attacking
him is that he must be sure in his own faith.

The second prayer, although short, is very much to
the point. The priest is not supposed to go to an
exorcism without being thoroughly conversant with the
complete ritual. It is one thing to read from a book in
the quietness of a room, but quite another to do so in
the macabre and often violent presence of the
possessed. So the suggestion is implanted that the book
of exorcism, or pontifical or missal should be read and
remembered. Neither is the priest to be influenced or
pass judgment on whether the possessed has been

baptized or not. As we know, this is generally taken care of later on.

In the third prayer the blessing is important because it acts as a shield for the priest. After all, he knows he is entering a battle and from the first is outnumbered by the afflicted one and the single or several demons that possess him.

The fourth prayer reiterates and emphasizes the points in all the preceding prayers.

The attitude of the Roman Catholic church seems clear. If there is work to be done—albeit unpleasant work, as exorcism surely is—then it is better to get on with the work. By acknowledging the fact that demons have power to direct material forces to their own evil ways, half the battle is assured. Exorcism becomes just another prayer to God in the name of all that is holy, and it is an act performed by His faithful servants.

This is a prosaic enough attitude, but it fits in very well with the many personal exorcisms for which the Roman Catholic church is well known. Everything used on the altar is blessed, dwelling places are blessed as well as churches and people. A blessing is not only a dedication to good but also a shield against evil and is a minor form of exorcism. Holy water is a mixture of exorcised water and exorcised salt.

In all blessings the name of God is said and His help sought to endow material things with a supernatural power to protect those who use them and guard them against assaults from the devil and his demons. If the Roman Catholic priest is a truly dedicated person, sure in his faith, the prayers by his bishop simply extend his ability and reiterate that he is not going into battle with the devil with inadequate equipment.

The liberal Catholic Church is neither Roman Catholic nor Protestant. The word "catholic" means universal, and the liberal Catholics do not rely on any administration from the Holy See of Rome. They are under the authority of the pope as Vicar of the Church of Christ. Sacraments are administered, but there is more freedom for members in both belief and interpretation of the faith. There is less self-abasement, no fear of everlasting hell, and many of the more terrifying aspects of Catholicism have been eliminated. Healing services are often performed regularly, aiming to attain a balance between mind, body and spirit. This service is also a form of exorcism. Evil is not regarded as a manifestation through materialism, but as misdirected energy. In an official exorcism the priest has more freedom to use other things, such as incense, in addition to invoking the help of Christ, the Son of God. The aim is to establish a personal link between the priest and the possessed.

I like the idea of trying to restore the imbalance, since one of the major evils of the world seems to be the devastating attacks by society to create an imbalance. The idea of selling sex through the advantages of using certain common products is a clear example of how a serious imbalance can be caused, and the liberal Catholic church is as much concerned with life as it *is* as it is aware of the necessity of saving souls.

Buddhism, which is gaining many youthful converts in this age, has never placed limitations on evil and good, although evil is seen as a negative force. The belief in demons is common in India, and was especially so when Buddha walked on the earth; but today the belief in demons is in low profile since minor demons

157

are believed to be as useful in certain circumstances as minor gods. In early Buddhism demons were considered a result of the accumulation of bad karma in past lives. In most religions demons are masculine; in the Buddhist religion Mara, or Satan, is certainly masculine, but the most evil spirits are his daughters, Desire, Unrest and Pleasure. There is also a number of other evil spirits—such as Rahu, the giant demon, and Raksasas—who are capable of assuming sirenlike forms tempting man to desire, unrest and pleasure.

Like other religions, Buddhism has a form of exorcism: repeating special sutras originally spoken by Buddha and so of ancient origin. By constantly repeating the sutras, the thought forms of harmony are projected on the possessed, who in time will be released from evil forces. This is known as an indirect method of exorcism; similar sutras are also said to combat sickness.

Buddhism comes in several distinct forms. As practiced in Thailand, Burma and Ceylon, it relies on its strength through meditation and quietness, so that serenity is obtained. Demonology is much more in evidence in China, Korea, Japan, Tibet and Mongolia. Both the demons themselves and the exorcism are much more fearsome. Demons are said to be capable of inflicting evil not only on the possessed human body but are capable of animating dead bodies. The ghost phenomenon is linked with aspects of demonology as well as with ancestral worship. There is an acceptance, especially among the Chinese demonologists, of a close relationship between such demons and human beings. Taoist priests control demons by the use of charms, amulets, talismans and incantations—working on the premise that prevention is better than cure.

Evil spirits can also inhabit places and inanimate

articles, and in the Chinese New Year celebrations there
are prayers for exorcism in which the demons
associated with the Old Year are formally cast out.
Dedicated Tibetan monks deliberately seek out demons
and challenge them, but such demons are part of man's
own illusions. In short he is wrestling with the evil parts
of himself and must win the battle if he is to gain purity
within his own spirit. The priest deliberately challeng-
ing demons knows he takes a risk. But he is gambling
with his own being, mind, body and soul.

If he fails, he knows he can become mad and even
die, but the alternative is supreme liberation. By casting
out the demons within himself, the priest can go on to
be a lama, a very holy man, and initiates will be brought
to him to undergo their own trials by demons. Since
death is acceptable as a form of release, there is never
likely to be the concern for the death of an initiate in
terms the Western mind can comprehend. Death brings
a second chance and hopefully the deceased comes back
more capable of dealing with his personal demons.

In Buddhism, unlike so many of the other great
religions, the question of exorcism becomes much more
the personal business of the possessed, and he has most
of the responsibility for excommunicating his own
demons, something of an Herculean task. I think that
Alexandra David-Neel sums up the attitude of Tibetans
in her book, *Magic and Magicians in Tibet:*

> Gods, demons, the whole universe,
> are but a mirage which exists in the mind,
> springs from it and sinks into it.

Man's acceptance of responsibility to himself is,
perhaps, the greatest phenomenon of all, and a

responsibility we in the West are not yet able to comprehend.

Protestantism is the overall name for certain Christian groups immediately or remotely related to the *Reformation*, the movement initiated by Martin Luther in 1529. The result was the rise and establishment of *Protestant* churches apart from Roman Catholicism. Martin Luther had his own battle with the devil, and it is reported he threw an inkpot at him and the devil disappeared. The word "Protestantism" is derived from the "protestation" made at the meeting of the Reichstag at Spires in 1529, by the minority of evangelical estates. Protestantism was the religious aspect of the general transition toward the institutions of democracy and capitalism. Public education became the political, economic and cultural aspect of the transition. Protestants are divided into many groups, whose unity stems from opposition to Roman Catholicism. There is insistence on the Bible as primary guidance, but there is also emphasis on the congregation as a religious cell and the universal priesthood of all believers. The right of private judgment is also an integral part of Protestantism.

Martin Luther saw no objection to the exorcism in the baptismal service and retained an abbreviated version in his own service in 1523. In 1526 it was further abbreviated and the exsuffatio was eliminated. This was the thrice-repeated breathing on the face of the child with the words "Depart from him, thou unclean spirit and give place to the Holy Spirit, the Paraclete." It was this exorcism rite that caused bitter controversy within the Lutheran ranks and brought reproach from the Calvinists. Finally, at the Cassel Conference of 1661, this type of exorcism was changed to a prayer for deliverance from the power of Satan. Gradually even that disappeared from the baptismal rites of the Protestant churches.

From personal observation I find that members of the Church of England, which is Protestant, are much more concerned with the dangers of possession than members of the numerous Protestant churches in the United States. Many leaders of the Church of England have for some years retained groups of men specially capable of performing exorcisms. Some twenty years ago the Bishop of Exeter made headlines in all the newspapers when he exorcized an entire household within his diocese. A London bishop, Dr. Gerald Ellison, appointed the Reverend Henry Cooper as his official exorcist to help churches in his diocese fight the forces of evil. When the Reverend Cooper is called out to a case, he first tries to seek a rational explanation for the phenomenon. If he still has any doubts, he calls in a doctor or psychiatrist. If no medical explanation is available, then—and only then—will he conduct the rite of exorcism.

The Reverend Christopher Neil-Smith has spent most of his life either preparing himself to perform exorcisms or actually doing them. He was trained by the late Reverend Gilbert Shaw. He works rather like a water diviner; if he feels an evil force, it manifests itself with a sensation like a sharp sting in his hands. As in all Protestant exorcism he calls upon Jesus Christ, is authoritative in his commands for the demon or devil to leave the body. He makes the sign of the cross and lays his hands on the possessed person. Through this, the evil force in the person receives the impact of the power

161

of God through his hands. The vibrations reach a climax and then gradually subside as the force is released. Dr. Neil-Smith says this is not a psychic reaction but the action of the Holy Spirit driving out the evil.

Canon John Pearce Higgins is a former Vice Provost of Southwark Cathedral. Before that he was vicar of a church in Pitney, England. For many years he has been a major voice in warning people of the dangers of evil forces taking over the body of a person or a place, and has performed many exorcisms.

The formula for exorcism within the rules of the Protestant churches may not be so ritualized and dramatic as those of the Roman Catholic church, but they are known to be very effective. What the Protestant churches have done is abbreviate the ancient rite of exorcism; it remains effective because the holy name of God and His Son Jesus Christ are called upon. There is no reliance on the names of the saints, such as we find in the Roman Catholic rites.

Fearlessness and the ability to command the departure of the evil spirits are important attributes of the rite, as is the preparation of the exorcist himself. Literally, he must go to an exorcism and be cleansed spiritually and mentally. The exorcism of the exorcist is a necessity and has become part of the definite training of the Protestant clergyman to obtain direct permission from his bishop to perform an exorcism. But he must attain spiritual detachment so that he can clearly define and observe if a case of possession truly justifies the rite of baptism. This is a recent amendment to the Canon Law. Exorcism by Protestant standards has its roots in the New Testament rather than the Old. The concept is one of deliverance, and the Lord's Prayer is part of the ritual. Few exorcisms are achieved in a single confrontation between the exorcist and the possessed. The Lord's Prayer may have to be said many, many times with the emphasis on "Deliver us from all evil." Ultimately the act of exorcism results in a battle of wills. A lot of stamina is needed on the part of the clergyman, so it is important that he continue with his prayers when he is away from the object of possession.

Every church has retained within it to a lesser or greater degree some provision to deal with possession. The attitude toward Satan, the devil and demons may vary, but the acknowledgement that evil forces are around—whether in a material or a psychic sense—is a reminder to us that possession is an undeniable fact. There is always hope that all evils have an antidote; and in this case the antidote is exorcism. The availability of means and rites is considerable, but the end product is the expulsion of the devil by any of his names and the retrieving of a human being from a living hell.

Chapter Eleven

Mass Possession

Anyone interested in studying possession will find literally thousands of recorded cases in every language and from every area of the world. Not a single race or culture has escaped contact with Satan, the devil or any number of demons whose names are, indeed, legion. One can think of any country, great or small and, given the inclination and the time, I guarantee there is a documented record of possession and exorcism. The period of time can be taken from pre-Christian days to the present era. Not too many cases have been made public, and the librarians of the great libraries of the world are sometimes reluctant to reveal documents.

In the British Museum, for instance, there are some dramatic accounts of possession and exorcism, but they are kept in the inner sanctum of the famous reference library. Several documents have to be signed before a reader can go from the main reference area to the inner sanctum. There is a guard on each door who insists on written authority being presented, as well as personal identification. The rare books and documents are kept under the watchful eyes of numerous active assistants in the inner sanctum. Once inside these remarkable archives, an entire new world opens up concerning possession. With time, patience and some knowledge of other languages, the wealth of literature spills out.

I left the British Museum in a state of wonder that so much has been recorded on the subject of exorcism, and even more wonder that the public has so little knowledge and awareness of it. There are many thousands of individual cases of possession, but there are also rare gems of mass possession, which becomes an epidemic form of evil, a regular cacophony of evil. Such mass possession seems to have occurred in small communities cut off from the mainstream of life. The majority of epidemics, for instance, have broken out in convents and monasteries, where, by reason of close and perpetual contact, the danger of evil spreading was as virulent as any contagious disease.

The most complete reference on mass possession is contained in the tome written by L. F. Calmeil, *De la folie considerée sous le point de vue pathologique, philosophique et judiciare.* The two volumes were published in Paris in 1845. Detailed accounts are available in most instances. Here is an abbreviated listing in chronological order:

1491–94. Nuns at Cambraim in the county of La Marche, near Hammone.

1551. At Uvertet.

1550–56. Mass possession in the cloisters of Saint Brigitt near Xanten.

1552. The inhabitants of the town of Hammone as a result of a smaller mass epidemic at Kintorp, near Strassburg.

1554. Eighty-four persons affected in Rome, including twenty-four converted Jewesses.

1560–64. An attack on the Nazareth Convent in Cologne.

1566. In this case, the number of children affected varies in several reports, but ranges from thirty to seventy. The Foundling Hospital in Amsterdam was the location, and the majority of those attacked were young boys.

1590. In Milan thirty nuns were possessed.

1593. A comparatively minor epidemic at Friedeberg in Neumark; about ten people were known to be affected.

1594. Another case of mass possession at Friedeberg. Eighty persons were involved.

1609–11. The convent of the Ursulines at Aix.

1613. The convent of St. Brigitte in Lille. Several of the nuns of this convent had heard of or witnessed cases of possession in Aix. Like a contagious epidemic, it spread to Lille.

1628. A convent of nuns in Madrid.

1632–38. The most famous case of mass possession took place at the convent of the Little Ursulines at Loudon. This epidemic spread to affect women in Chinon, Nimes and Avignon. In Avignon, Cardinal Mazarin gave instructions that no one should discuss the cases and no publicity be given to possessed persons. This seems to have reduced the number of cases.

1642. Eighteen sisters of a convent in Louviers became affected.

1652–62. In ten years numerous cases of mass possession were recorded and took place in a convent at Auzonne.

1670. Many children in Mora, Sweden, were the victims.

1670. An orphanage at Hoorn, Holland. Children of both sexes affected, all under the age of twelve.

1681. Several cases were reported in the area of Toulouse.

1687–90. Fifty sisters were victims in a convent in Lyon.

1732. A minor epidemic near Bayeux.

1740–50. Another lengthy and persistent epidemic in a convent at Unterzell in Lower Franconia.

1857–62. About one hundred and twenty people were demonically attacked at Morzines, a small village in the Haute Savoie region, then very cut off from civilization.

1878. A minor epidemic at Verzegnis.

1881. The neighborhood of St. Brieuc became victims.

1881. Another minor epidemic at Jaca in Spain.

The most famous case of mass possession took place at Loudon. It has been remarkably well recorded and has been the subject of a movie called *Mother Joan of the Angels*, produced and directed by the Polish filmmaker, Kawalerowic. The late Aldous Huxley also wrote a book about the devils of Loudon.

It seems safe to conclude that environment plays a major part in all cases of mass possession, but interior tendencies and even trivia make a contribution. Father Surin, who played a major and ultimately tragic role in observing and exorcising the demons of Loudon, also gives a full description of it in his *Histoire des diables de Loudon*. He states that one day the demons cast a spell on the Mother Prioress, so that she became a different person. For eight days "her face shone with rare beauty." Then "on another day the demons assumed my appearance, entered the parlor and speaking in a soft voice which had some semblance to mine, attempted to lead the same Mother Prioress into temptation. The Ursuline nuns, like stricken birds, attempted to exorcise the evil. . . ."

The possession went on for six years, with 1635 as the most dramatic year, and the highest number of cases were recorded. Father Surin was called on to perform many of the exorcisms. When he presented himself at the Ursuline convent, the Prioress was totally possessed and the symptoms were spreading to the nuns. The Prioress, Sister Jean des Anges, however, was able to analyze her own guilt obsession with remarkable clarity. She stated: "I was nearly always suffering from remorse of conscience and with good reason. The devil acted in me only in proportion as I allowed him entry. Demons took possession of all my exterior and interior faculties to do their will with me. Not because I believe myself to be guilty of blasphemy and other disorders into which the devils often cast me, but because in the beginning I listened to their suggestions."

The Prioress blasphemed against God, insulted his angels and saints, expressed her hatred of religious life, tore and chewed upon her vestments and spat out the Host while insulting the priest. There were days when she was able to resist the devils, but they became comparatively few in the six years of possession. Sometimes she admitted that she wanted to submit to possession and that she even enjoyed it. "The devil often tricked me by a little feeling of pleasure that I had in the disturbances and other extraordinary things he occassioned in my heart."

Jeanne des Anges left an autobiography, although it

cannot be considered the best evidence available since it is obvious that she entered the convent with a weak moral nature and an inclination to hysteria. She was not suited to a life of religious devotion and must have felt considerable resentfulness, thus laying the foundation for any demon to enter her. Added to this was her own desire to be possessed, probably as revenge for being sent to the convent. In her autobiography, entitled *Bibliotheque diabolique,* she says (page 65):

At the commencement of my possession I was almost three months in a continued disturbance of mind so that I do not remember anything of what passed during that time. The demons acted with abounding force and the church fought them day and night with exorcisms. My mind was often filled with blasphemies, and sometimes I uttered them without being able to take any thought to stop myself. I felt for God a continual aversion and nothing inspired me with greater hatred than the spectacle of his goodness and the readiness with which he pardons repentant sinners. My thoughts were often bent on devising ways to displease him and to make others trespass against him. It is true that by the mercy of God, I was not free in these sentiments, although at that time I did not know it, for the demon beclouded me in such a way that I hardly distinguished his desires from mine; he gave me, moreover, a strong aversion for my religious calling, so that sometimes when he was in my head, I tore my veils and such of my sisters' as I could lay hands on; I trampled them underfoot, I chewed them, cursing the hour when I took the vows. All this was done with great violence; I think I was not free. As I went up for Communion, the devil took possession of my hand and when I received the Sacred Host and had half moistened it, the devil flung it into the priest's face. I know full well that I did not do this action freely, but I am fully assured to my deep confusion that I gave the devil occasion to do it. I think he would not have had the power if I had not been in league with him. I have on several other occasions had similar experiences, for when I resisted them stoutly, I found that all these furies and rages dispersed as they had come, but, alas, it too often happened that I did not strongly constrain myself in little things, especially in matters where I saw no grievous sin. But this is where I deluded myself, for because I did not restrain myself in little things my mind was afterwards taken unawares in great ones.

At this reply, the evil spirit got into such a fury that I thought he would kill me; he beat me with great violence so that my face was quite disfigured and my body all bruised with his blows.

It often happened that he treated me in this way.

As for outward things I think I was much troubled by almost continual rages and fits of madness. I found myself almost incapable of doing any good things, seeing that I had not an hour of the liberty to think of my conscience and prepare myself for general confession, although God caused me to be moved toward it and I was so minded.

But the real tragedy of Loudon was not the Prioress, who lived to recover from her possession, but the gentle ascetic Father Surin. He became the ultimate sacrifice to the devil. Surin sent several pathetic letters to a friend. The first one was written on May 3, 1635. A version of this remarkable letter appeared in a book by an unknown author called Aubin. The title of the work is *Les Cruels effets de la vengeance du Cardinal Richelieu ou Histoire des diables de Loudon.* Since Father Surin refers to his friend as "Your Reverence," it can be presumed that he was writing to a spiritual mentor. Extracts from the lengthy epistle are as follows:

I am no longer at Mareenes but at Loudon. I am in perpetual conversation with the devils. . . .

I have engaged in combat with four of the most potent and malicious devils in hell. I, I say, whose infirmities you know. God has permitted the struggles to be so fierce and the onslaughts so frequent that exorcism was the least of the battlefields, for the enemies declared themselves in private both by day and night in a thousand different ways. You can imagine what pleasure there is in finding oneself at the sole mercy of God. For the last three months and a half I have never been without a devil working upon me.

Things have gone so far that God has permitted, I think for my sins, what has perhaps never been seen in the church, that in the exercise of my ministry, the devil passes out of the body of the possessed woman and entering into mine assaults and confounds me, agitates and troubles me visibly, possessing me for several hours like a demoniac. I cannot explain to you what happens within me during this time and how this spirit unites with mine, without depriving me either of consciousness or liberty of soul, nevertheless making himself like another me and as if I had two souls, one of which is dispossessed of its body and the use of its organs and stands aside watching the actions of the other, which has entered into them. The two spirits fight in one and the same field, which is the body, and the victim is as if divided. According to one of its parts it is subject to diabolic impressions and according to the other to those motions which are proper to it or granted by God. . . .

Father Surin goes on to say:

> I feel the state of damnation and apprehend it and feel
> myself as if transpierced with arrows of despair in that
> stranger soul which seems to be mine, while the other
> soul which is full of confidence laughs at such feelings
> and is at full liberty to curse him who is the cause. The
> tremblings which I feel when the Holy Sacrament is
> administered to me arise equally, as far as I can judge,
> from horror of its presence which is insufferable to me
> and from a sincere and meek reverence, without it
> being possible for me to attribute them to the one rather
> than the other or to check them. When I desire by the
> motion of one of these two souls to make the sign of the
> cross on my mouth, the other averts my hand with great
> swiftness and grips my fingers in its teeth to bite me with
> rage. I scarcely ever find orisons easier or more tranquil
> than in these agitations; when the body rolls upon the
> ground and the ministers of the church speak to me as
> to a devil, loading me with maledictions, I cannot tell
> you of the joy I feel, having become a devil not by
> rebellion against God but by the calamity which shows
> me plainly the state to which sin has reduced me, and
> how that taking to myself all the curses which are
> heaped on me my soul has reason to sink in its own
> nothingness. When the other possessed persons see me
> in this state, it is a pleasure to see how they triumph and
> how the devils mock at me saying, "Physician heal
> thyself! Go now and climb into the pulpit, it will be a fine
> sight to see him preach after he has rolled on the
> ground!"

That which I am is such that I can do few things
freely, when I wish to speak my speech is cut off; at Mass
I am brought up short; at table I cannot carry the
morsel to my mouth; at confession I suddenly forget my

sins; and I feel the devil come and go within me as if he were at home. As soon as I wake he is there, at orisons he distracts my thoughts when he pleases; when my heart begins to swell with the presence of God, he fills me with rage; he makes me sleep when I would wake; and publicly, by the mouth of the possessed woman, he boasts of being my master; the which I can in no way contradict. It is not a single demon who torments me, there are usually two; one is the Leviathan, the adversary of the Holy Spirit, for according to what they have said here, they have in hell a trinity whom the magicians worship: Lucifer, Beelzebub and Leviathan, who is third in hell, as some authors have already observed and written. Now the works of this false Paraclete are quite contrary to those of the true and impart a desolation which cannot be adequately described. He is the chief of all our band of demons and has command of this whole affair which is perhaps one of the strangest ever seen. In this same place we see Paradise and Hell, nuns who are taken in one way like Ursula and in the other worse than the most abandoned in all sorts of disorder, filth, blasphemy and rages.

Father Surin ends this part of his letter by asking his spiritual friend to respect it as confidential. In a postscript he asks for prayers to be said for him and says that he is content to die, believing that the devil will not desist within him until he has achieved his death.

There are several as yet unpublished letters from Father Surin to his spiritual adviser; these are in the original manuscript form in the archives of the Bibliothèque Nationale of Paris.

Surin achieved a certain amount of success with his exorcisms, and it is known that the Prioress profited from his ministrations. But he himself lapsed from one form of depression to another, complaining all the time of the dual spirits within him. His torments lasted for twenty-five years. Finally he lost the power of movement and his speech. He fell into a sickness "unknown to doctors whose remedies were of no avail." On several occasions he attempted suicide but finally came to believe that it was by the will of God that he should remain among the damned. He died violently and left behind the legacy of an enigma of dual personality and possession.

But the story of the diabolic possession of the nuns of Loudon has another story within it, actually a possible curtain raiser to the diabolic events as they unfolded. The year before these possessions took place, a libertine priest called Urbain Grandier was burned at the stake for practicing witchcraft. Grandier was a curate of St. Pierre du Marche, the parish church of Loudon. He had the ability to mesmerize his congregation and was handsome, vain and very much of an antihero. He seduced the local virgins as well as lonely widows and led a far-from-exemplary life by any standard. But he was not the monster some writers have tried to make him out to be.

He might have gone on with his work as curate and unofficial Lothario if he had not made the mistake of insulting the all-powerful, politically conscious Cardinal Richelieu. He attacked the cardinal on a matter of church protocol in 1624, and we know the first possession at the Ursuline convent occurred in 1632. What could be more natural than that the cardinal should cause him to be accused of bewitching the nuns.

By this means the cardinal—known for his cunning methods—could kill two birds with one stone. The nuns of Loudon were an embarassment to the church and were a public spectacle since tens of thousands of people from all over France came to see their behavior in the Church of Saint Croix. Secondly, by accusing Grandier of witchcraft, the cardinal could dispose of an enemy without any blame to himself.

The witch hunters of Loudon subjected Grandier to horrible torture; finally they crushed his legs and burned him at the stake on August 18, 1634. The curate was courageous to the end and stanchly proclaimed his innocence.

At that time Loudon had a population of 20,000, and the reason for Cardinal Richelieu's interest was that the city was the stronghold of many proud Huguenot families. They outnumbered the Roman Catholics and thus presented a threat to the influence of the cardinal. He destroyed Grandier as an example of his power and then destroyed the fortified castle, a stronghold of the Huguenots.

The city was cursed by Grandier and, indeed, it seemed the curse had effect. The city was ravaged by plagues, while counterreformation groups diminished the central power invested in the Roman Catholics over the feudal fiefdoms; after such devastation the city never regained its importance. There is not a single Protestant family in the city today. The descendants of the judges who sentenced Grandier to death all died extraordinarily disagreeable deaths.

The possession of the nuns continued, and it was gaining strength in 1635 at the time when Father Surin wrote the epistle to his spiritual friend. Today there is still an official Roman Catholic exorcist resident in the town whose population is now only 8,000 souls.

There are only a few stones left of the Ursuline convent, but there is a sign that indicates the Street of the Rack. Dominating the square where Grandier was burned is the Church of Saint Croix where the famous exorcism took place. He paid the penalty not for his own arrogance and earthly misdemeanors, but because he challenged the power of the cardinal, who was once called the most powerful man in France. The town has been modernized, but the memories of Loudon remain as the city of possessed nuns, endowed with the curse of Grandier.

Nineteenth-century author and poet Sir Walter Scott wrote a historical survey of demonology in England called *Letters on Demonology and Witchcraft in England.* This work is probably better known today than when it was first published in 1830, and it includes a few accounts of possession. One relates a case of mass possession in America.

The first case which I observed was that of four children of a person called John Goodwin, a mason. The eldest, a girl, had quarreled with the laundress, an ignorant, testy and choleric old Irishwoman scolded the accuser; and shortly afterwards, the elder Goodwin, her sister and two brothers were seized with such strange diseases that all their neighbors concluded they were bewitched. They conducted themselves as those supposed to suffer under such maladies created by such influence were accustomed to do. They stiffened their necks so hard at one time that the joints could not be moved; at another time their necks were so flexible and supple that it seemed the bone was dissolved. They had violent convulsions, in which their jaws snapped with the force of a spring trap set for vermin. Their limbs were curiously distorted and, to those who had a taste for the marvellous, seemed entirely dislocated and displaced. Amid these distortions, they cried out against the poor old woman, whose name was Glover, alleging that she was in presence with them, adding to their torments. The miserable Irishwoman, who hardly could speak the English language, repeated her Pater Noster and Ave Maria like a good Catholic; but there were some words which she had forgotten. She was therefore supposed to be unable to pronounce the whole consistently and correctly, and condemned and executed accordingly. But the children of Goodwin found the trade they were engaged in too profitable to be laid aside and the eldest in particular continued all the external signs of witchcraft and possession. Some of these were excellently calculated to flatter the self opinion and prejudices of the Calvinist ministers, by whom she was attended, and accordingly bear in their very front, the character of studied and voluntary imposture. The young woman, acting as was supposed, under the influence of the Devil, read a Quaker treatise with ease and apparent satisfaction; but a book written against the poor inoffensive Friends, the Devil would not allow his victim to touch. She could look on a Church of England Prayer Book and read portions of the Scriptures which it contains, without difficulty or impediment; but the spirit which possessed her threw her into fits if she attempted to read the same Scripture from the Bible, as if the awe which it is supposed the fiends entertain for the Holy Writ depended, not on meanings of words but the arrangement of the page,

and the type in which they were printed. This singular
form of flattery was designed to captivate the clergyman
through his professional opinions.

Unfortunately Sir Walter Scott does not give the
source of this episode, except to set the scene in
America. Cases of epidemic possession were known in
America at the time when Scott wrote his *Demonology*.
One of the most notorious cases of mass possession took
place in Salem Village, Massachusetts, a rural community some distance from Salem proper, which is now
named Danvers. Mass cases of possession always seem to
be associated with witchcraft, and the Salem case is
known historically as "The Salem Witches."

It is very doubtful if any of the possessed people knew
anything about witchcraft, although they must certainly
have been aware of black magic. A group of eight girls,
whose ages ranged from eleven to twenty, was
accustomed to meet in the minister's house, and there
they met the minister's slave, a woman named Tituba, a
native of Barbados. It is more than likely that she
regaled the young girls with stories of voodoo and black
magic as practiced in the West Indies.

The first girl to succumb to possession was Abigail,
the youngest girl, who was related to the Reverend
Samuel Parris. She lived in his house and was therefore
constantly in the company of Tituba. Her friend, Ann
Putnam, also succumbed and the two girls acted as if
they had been transformed into animals, moaning and
writhing on the ground while uttering obscenities. The
symptoms spread to the other young people.

The minister, in his capacity as spiritual adviser and
relation of one of the victims, decided to find out who

had bewitched the children and caused them to be possessed. He called in an Indian medicine man, but he revealed nothing to the minister.

Then in February of 1692, Abigail and Ann accused three people of being responsible for the possession. The people named were Tituba, Sarah Good and Sarah Osbourne. The two last named were not exactly the most popular people in the community and had already incurred the distrust and disapproval of the Puritan settlement. The women were arrested on March 1; the two Sarahs staunchly denied involvement, but Tituba confessed that she and others had been in league with Satan. When exposed to the three accused, the girls went into spasms in which limbs and facial muscles were distorted.

Although she confessed, Tituba was never brought to trial and was subsequently sold by Mr. Parris to defray the costs of the court case; Sarah Osbourne died while awaiting trial. Meanwhile all the girls began to name people as being responsible for their torment. Those who confessed and implicated others were allowed their freedom, but those who maintained their innocence were brought to trial and condemned. These included the Reverend George Burroughs, Martha Corey, a member of the church, and Rebecca Nurse, an invalid who had up to that time had an unsullied reputation. Bridget Bishop and Susanna Martin were elderly villagers who were believed to have been involved in witchcraft before, and so were naturally suspect.

The trial started in June and those indicted were brought before a special commission of judges appointed by Sir William Phips. All through the trial the young girls continued to show signs of possession at the sight of the accused. One wonders why they were exposed to the accused, but I suppose it was necessary for the children to give evidence at the trial. There was no evidence of any substance against Rebecca Nurse and she was found not guilty; but the court reversed the decision of the jury. With Sarah Good, Susanna Martin and three others, Rebecca was hanged on July 19.

Having gone so far, there was no point of return for the court and jury. To admit they might have made a mistake would have made them objects of derision or worse still, be accused of being accessories of the devil. So the trials continued. Martha Corey and May Easty, the sister of Rebecca Nurse, were also executed.

It was a summer of panic in Salem Village, and the fever spread as Abigail and Ann persisted in accusing people, literally at random. They made history as the youngest people ever to gain reputations as witch hunters. This reputation gradually gained ground over their reputation of being possessed. The nearby town of Andover invited the girls to point out any witches that may have been lurking within that settlement. It is horrible to think that the children never left without finding people to denounce as witches.

The court was working hard on convictions, but was eager to add other accusations to the original one of being in league with the devil and causing possession. In August George Burroughs was hanged with John Willard, the first of the Andover crop. In September Giles Corey, the eighty-year-old husband of Martha, was also accused; he refused to plead either guilty or not guilty. In those days a trial could not take place unless the accused pleaded one way or the other. In order to "persuade" Giles Corey to plead, he was subjected to torture—in this case a particularly disgusting one. He was forced to lie on the floor of his cell while heavy weights were put on his body. Old and frail, he succumbed to his torture, but at least he died uncondemned by a court of law and so his worldly goods were not confiscated by the state.

By September 22, 1692, twenty people had been hanged and some two hundred had been accused by the girls. Fortunately Governor Phips returned in October and cancelled the commissioned court, although some of the accused remained in prison until the end of the year. Months of arguments about the influence of Satan and his possession of the eight girls took place. The well-recorded events of the possessions and witchcraft trials at Salem Village remain a blot on the judicial system of the times as well as the bigoted theology of the Puritans.

After the trials there was a change of opinion among villagers and those in the surrounding district. Thomas Brattle, a merchant from Boston, became the champion of reason, with many people on his side. His activities resulted in a further state of upset initiated by Cotton Mather. In 1693 he published *The Wonder of the Invisible World*. Brattle firmly believed that the devil was the main persecutor of the possessed girls and the cause of their afflictions. As far as Mather was concerned, Salem Village had practically been homesteaded by Satan during the summer of 1692.

The witch hunt in Massachusetts was small in comparison to those that took place in Europe. That the girls were possessed by the devil I have no doubt, but the evil was in them by their own desire and not by the influence of people who had little or no consciousness of witchcraft. Salem Village held a day of mourning for the victims, and the state made retribution to the heirs of the accused. The girls recovered and probably never knew that their possession made history. The devil had had his holiday in Salem Village in the black summer of 1692. In 1953 the events were immortalized by Arthur Miller in his prize-winning play *The Crucible*.

Cases of mass possession emphasize the trail of misery that stretches out into the lives of the innocent. In single cases of possession the misery and diabolic effects are restricted and are almost always subjected to exorcism. The mass possession of Salem Village was unique because no one seemed to think about exorcising the children, although the settlement was strongly Puritan. Indeed, it is remarkable that the devil was adventurous enough to move into a settlement already renowned for its religious zeal. Perhaps it was the ultimate challenge; the result seems to have been one of the few victories for Satan. Not only did he possess the young girls, but his evil influence finally echoed in the lives of all the villagers. They were the guilty ones—not the poor souls who were hanged.

Chapter Twelve

All This, and Hell, Too !

I believe in the power of names and that each name sets up a vibration and is more than the distinguishing appelation by which a person, place or thing is known. At one time great thought and consideration were given to the choice of a name.

Primitive tribes have probably more awareness of the importance of a name—more than we have in sophisticated society. The American Indians used names that ultimately gave a clue to what was expected of the child. He had something to live up to if he were called Great Hunter. The Anglo-Saxons followed the same principle in giving names such as Ethelwulf, meaning Noble Wolf. Many native societies give their children two names, one for everyday use and one as a spiritual name. True, there is some concern that by giving two names the evil spirits will become confused. Those entering religious orders are given new names, and in Wicca, all initiated members have a special witch-name.

In exorcism we know that the calling out of the name of the highest deity is an important factor in forcing the devil to relinquish his hold on a possessed person. Yet today we use the name of God and Jesus Christ very indiscriminately and sometimes as a form of expletive. More amazing still, we use the word "devil" just as frequently. In the twentieth century the devil is more on the social scene than anyone else. He has been dramatized on the stage and in operas, as well as providing the central character for many books. I know several families who call their household pets either Satan or Devil, and "you little devil" is almost a term of endearment when applied to a child or even an adult. We speak of adopting a "devil-may-care" attitude, which erroneously implies that the devil is capable of caring—which seems to be diametrically opposite to the most notable characteristics of the adversary of the All-Caring God.

Piously we say, "The devil finds work for idle hands," and hope it will frighten young people into seeing work as a major attribute of life and a means of salvation. "The little devil in your eyes" has been a mainstay of lyricists who have become bored with rhyming "moon" with "June." The bogeyman used by Victorian parents as a ploy to scare their offspring was really the devil in a sanctimonious disguise. The devil is always at the tip of our tongue, right there at the very orifice through which he loves to enter the body. Although we no longer believe (or do we?) that the devil is responsible for all sicknesses, it is not unusual for someone to say, "The pain is like a thousand devils tearing at my guts," or that something "hurts like the devil."

By such frequent usage the names Old Nick, alias Satan, alias Lucifer the Prince of Light, alias Ashmodeus, we make our own contribution to keeping him alive. Even in law courts and on television interviews the devil is still with us as someone decides to become "the devil's adversary"—that is, a provoker, catalyst designed to reveal or conceal a deceit. In tight moments, when we feel trapped, we are encouraged to "run like the devil," and to "fight like the devil" is practically an accolade. We eat devil's food cake and invent drinks in the name of His Satanic Majesty.

There is as much folklore, mythology, poetic inspiration and awareness of the devil as there is for God. By any name the devil is likely to set up fears within us, but we certainly make good use of his name. Go to any costume party and who are you certain to meet? Why, your neighbor dressed up as the devil, complete with horns, tail and pitchfork. I never went to such a party and saw anyone dressed up as God or Jesus Christ! The devil is the consistent partygoer and generally the life and soul of the occasion, which is just about as strange a description as any I can think of!

The devil is also a big moneymaker. Give him a star role in a movie or a book and then listen for the cash registers emulating perpetual motion. There are alarms and excursions sounded when the devil is placed on exhibition through the magic of the silver screen. Once there was an outcry because someone said, "God is dead"; now we have hysteria because the devil is alive and doing very nicely throughout every city and village where there is a moviehouse. Petitions are signed to close those cinemas where the devil is having a ball, and theologians thunder from their pulpits; psychologists get almost as rich as doctors by the spin-off results from people paying to see films they know will horrify them. Come to think of it, I never saw anyone hog-tied and dragged screaming *into* a cinema. Those who want to see the devil in his diabolic antics go willingly, like sheep to the slaughterhouse, standing in line, waiting patiently to be stunned into a new form of neurosis or hysteria.

Two high-voltage names in music, Jerome Robbins and composer-conductor Leonard Bernstein, have completed a new ballet derived from the classic Yiddish play, *The Dybbuk*. The possessed and the devil in ballet slippers should capture any intellectuals who may have missed being ensnared by possession and exorcism on film.

Although the logical abode for the devil is hell, we have named many exceptionally beautiful and unique places after him. In Wales he has a famous bridge; in Colorado, a gate; a kitchen in New York; a peak in Oregon; a tower in Wyoming; a point on Catalina Island; a slide in Utah; a punchbowl in England; a river in Texas; a hole in the North Sea; a paw in British Columbia; an elbow in Scotland (and another in Alaska); a gorge in Zambia; and, naturally, a playground in California.

We fear the devil, despise him, pray for protection from him—but we are quick enough to give him his due even if it's only a name. Without such homage, no doubt there would be the devil to pay! Several dozen plants are named after him, including the Devil's Snuffbox, otherwise known as the puffball. There are apples for the devil, aprons, bushes, candlesticks, coachwheels, cotton, ears, figs, horns, leaves, oatmeal and toadstools, and if the devil had to pay his own dues, he could do it with devil's gold or employ his own printer to make pamphlets.

Any gambler drawing the four of clubs calls it the

devil's bedpost, and such a gambler would never know the devil's own luck because such a card denotes a loss at poker, solo whist and other card games. Should the gambler then turn to the crap table, he can roll the devil's cones, better known as dice. The devil plays, acts and does remarkable things with eggs and many a person not yet ready for Alcoholics Anonymous can be as drunk as the devil—and as a prank he can hold a candle to the same devil.

We can talk of the devil and be sure he will appear, but even this is not sufficient warning. In 1771 an unknown poet summed it all up. The poem is bad, but the message is for us today:

> Forthwith the devil did appear,
> For name him and he's always near.

Considering the devil is an outcast, a veritable antihero in this day of nonheroes, as a potential claimant to the role of the past, present and future anti-Christ, the devil has done very well for himself. But we are his public-relations agency; we know him, name him, call upon him and then profess surprise when he appears. He is possessive, aggressive and demanding enough to want the ultimate gift to add to his frightening shower of goodies, and that is a human body and mind to play around in and another soul for Satan. Hell was never enough for the devil, and nothing seems to have changed today.

"The force of an exorcism," says Origen (the distinguished theologian who lived c185–c254), "lies in the name of Jesus, which is spoken and in which his Gospels are proclaimed." The early Christians knew the

187

value of a "name-spell" and Origen again expresses this most adequately.

> And thus it is not the thing signified, but the qualities and peculiarities of words which possess a certain power for this or that purpose.

When you blurt out the old cliche, "What's in a name?" take care, because the devil loves recognition. Apparently he gets it, too, as we can see in the following references to the devil and Satan in the literature of the world.

> One more devils'-triumph and sorrow
>   for angels,
> One more wrong to man, one more insult
>   to God!
> > Robert Browning (1841–1846)
> > *Bells and Pomegranates*

> Get thee behind me, Satan.
> > Matthew XVI:23

> Tell your master that if there were as many devils at Worms as tiles on its roofs, I would enter.
> > Martin Luther (1483–1546)
> > *On Approaching Worms*

> To consume your own choler, as some chimneys consume their own smoke; to keep a whole Satanic School spouting, if it must spout, inaudibly, is a negative yet no slight virtue, nor one of the commonest in these times.
> > Thomas Carlyle (1795–1881)
> > *Sartor Resartus*, Book II

The Devil was sick,—the Devil a
  monk would be;
The Devil was well,—the Devil a
  monk was he.
> François Rabelais (1495–1553)
> *Works,* Book II, Chap. 24

Satan came also.
> Job I:6

He cursed him in sleeping, that every night
He should dream of the devil, and wake in a fright.
> Richard Harris Barham
> (1788–1845)
> *Ingoldsby Legends. The Jackdaw of*
> *Rheims*

And was Jerusalem builded here
Among those dark Satanic mills?
> William Blake (1757–1827)
> *Milton,* Stanza 2

Here's the devil-and-all to pay.
> Miguel de Cervantes (1547–1616)
> *Don Quixote,* Part I, Book IV,
> Chap. 10

Once, early in the morning,
  Beelzebub arose,
With care his sweet person adorning,
  He put on his Sunday clothes.
> Percy Bysshe Shelley (1792–1822)
> *The Devil's Walk, A Ballad,* Stanza I

The Devil enters the prompter's box
  and the play is ready to start.

189

Robert William Service
(1874-1958)
The Harpy, Stanza 12

Hee must have a long spoon, shall eat with the devill.
John Heywood
Proverbs (1546) Part II, Chap. V

Abash'd the devil stood,
And felt how awful goodness is, and saw
Virtue in her shape how lovely.
John Milton (1608–74)
Paradise Lost, Book IV,
Line 846

You are pictures out of doors,
Bells in your parlours, wild-cats in your kitchens
Saints in your injuries, devils being offended,
Players in your housewifery, and housewives
in your beds.
William Shakespeare
(1564–1616)
Othello, Act II, Sc. 1, Line 109

And the Lord said unto Satan,
Whence comest thou? Then Satan answered
the Lord, and said, From going to and fro
in the earth, and from walking up and down
in it.
Job I:7

Out of his surname they have coined an epithet for a
knave, and out of his Christian name a synonym for the
Devil.
Thomas Babington Macaulay
Machiavelli (1827)

The art of life is to keep down acquaintances. One's friends one can manage, but one's acquaintances can be the devil.

Edward Verrall Lucas
(1868–1938)
Over Bremerton's

Satan now is wiser than of yore,
And tempts by making rich, not making poor.

Alexander Pope (1688–1744)
Moral Essays, Epistle III,
Line 351

And the Devil did grin, for his darling sin
Is pride that apes humility.

Samuel Taylor Coleridge
(1772–1834)
The Devil's Thoughts

High on a throne of royal state, which far
Outshone the wealth of Ormus and of Ind,
Or where the gorgeous East with richest hand
Showers on her kings barbaric pearl and gold,
Satan exalted sat, by merit rais'd
To that bad eminence.

John Milton (1608–1674)
Paradise Lost, Book II, Line 1

Resist the Devil, and he will flee from you.

James IV:7

The Devil hath not, in all his quiver's choice,
An arrow for the heart like a sweet voice.

George Gordon, Lord Byron
(1788–1824)
Don Juan, Canto XV, Stanza 13

There are in every man, at every hour, two simultaneous postulations, one toward God, the other toward Satan.

> Charles Baudelaire (1821–1867)
> *Mon Coeur Mis à Nu*, XIX

Black as the devil,
Hot as hell,
Pure as an angel,
Sweet as love.

> Charles Maurice
>   de Talleyrand-Périgord
> (1754–1838)
> *Recipe for Coffee*

The devil damn thee black, thou cream-faced loon!
Where gott'st thou that goose look?
> William Shakespeare
> *Macbeth*, Act V, Sc. 3, Line 11

For Satan finds some mischief still
For idle hands to do.
> Nicholas Rowe (1673–1718)
> *Divine Songs*, XX

Omnis festinatio est a diabolo.
All haste is from the devil.
> Medieval Latin proverb

We returned from the Pole to Cape Columbia in only sixteen days . . . the exhilaration of success lent wings to our sorely battered feet. But Ootah, the Eskimo, had his own explanation. Said he: "The devil is asleep or having trouble with his wife, or we should never have come back so easily."

Robert Edwin Peary
(1856–1920)
The North Pole

Be sober, be vigilant; because your adversary,
the Devil, as a roaring lion, walketh about, seeking
whom he may devour.
I Peter V:8

A limb of Satan.
Mark Twain (Samuel
Langhorne Clemens)
(1835–1910)
Life on the Mississippi, Chap. 8

The fiend with all his comrades
Fell then from heaven above,
Through as long as three nights and days,
The angels from heaven into hell;
And them all the Lord transformed to devils,
Because they his deed and word
Would not revere.
Caedmon (*Floruit* 670)
*Creation. The Fall of
the Rebel Angels*

Go, poor devil, get thee gone! Why should
I hurt thee? This world surely is wide enough
to hold both thee and me.
Laurence Sterne (1713–68)
Tristram Shandy, Book II,
Chap. 12

Sometimes we are devils to ourselves
When we will tempt the frailty of our powers,
Presuming on their changeful potency.

193

William Shakespeare
Troilus and Cressida, Act IV,
Sc. 4, Line 95

Every man for himself, his own ends, the Devil for all.
Robert Burton (1577–1640)
Anatomy of Melancholy
Part III, Sect. I, Memb. III

Had there been a Lunatic Asylum in the suburbs of Jerusalem, Jesus Christ would infallibly have been shut up in it at the outset of his public career. That interview with Satan on a pinnacle of the Temple would alone have damned him, and everything that happened after could but have confirmed the diagnosis.
Havelock Ellis (1859–1939)
Impressions and Comments,
Series III

Wherever God erects a house of prayer,
The Devil always builds a chapel there;
And 'twill be found, upon examination,
The latter has the largest congregation.
Daniel Defoe (1661–1731)
The True-Born Englishman,
Part I, Line I

. . . that devil's madness—War.
Robert William Service
(1874–1958)
Michael

Renounce the devil and all his works, the vain pomp and glory of the world, with all covetous desires of the same, and the sinful desires of the flesh.
Book of Common Prayer

194

American Revision, 1928
Holy Baptism. Of Children

The Devil himself, which is the author of confusion and lies.

Robert Burton (1577–1640)
Anatomy of Melancholy.
Sect. 4, Memb. 1, Subsect. 3

The lunatic, the lover, and the poet
Are of imagination all compact:
One sees more devils than vast hell
   can hold,
That is, the madman . . .

William Shakespeare
A Midsummer Night's Dream,
Act V, Sc. 1, Line 7

Three faces wears the doctor: when first sought
An Angel's; and a god's the cure half-wrought;
But when, the cure complete, he seeks his fee,
The Devil looks less terrible than he.

Anonymous

The heart of man is the place the devils dwell in:
I feel sometimes a hell within myself.

Sir Thomas Browne (1605–82)
Religio Medici, Part I, Sect. LI

An apology for the Devil: It must be remembered that we have only heard one side of the case. God has written all the books.

Samuel Butler (1835–1902)
Note-Books. Higgledy-Piggledy:
An Apology for the Devil

195

Talk of the devil, and his horns appear, says the proverb.

> Samuel Taylor Coleridge
> (1772–1834)
> *Biographia Literaria*, Chap. 23

He's a very devil.

> Shakespeare
> *Twelfth Night*, Act III, Sc. 4,
> Line 304

You're a devil at everything; and there's no kind of thing in the versal world but what you can turn your hand to.

> Miguel de Cervantes
> (1547–1616)
> *Don Quixote*. Part I, Book III,
> Chap. 11, Page 196

The Devil must be in that little Jackdaw!

> Richard Harris Barham
> (1788–1845)
> *Ingoldsby Legends*
> *The Jackdaw of Rheims*

Go, and catch a falling star,
  Get with child a mandrake root,
Tell me, where all past years are,
  Or who cleft the Devil's foot.

> John Donne (1573–1631)
> *Song*, Stanza 1

The Devil whispered behind the leaves,
"It's pretty, but is it Art?"

> Rudyard Kipling (1865–1936)
> *The Conundrum of the Workshops*

Your new-caught, sullen peoples,
Half-devil and half-child.
> Rudyard Kipling
> *The White Man's Burden*

God sends meat, and the Devil sends cooks.

> John Taylor (1578–1653)
> *Works* (1630), Vol. II

"I should count myself the coward if I left them,
my Lord Howard,
To these Inquisition dogs and the devildoms of Spain."
> Alfred, Lord Tennyson
> (1809–92)
> *The Revenge*, Stanza 2

So over violent, or over civil,
That every man with him was God or Devil.
> John Dryden (1631–1700)
> *Absalom and Achitophel*,
> Part I, Line 557

The stars move still, time runs, the clock will strike,
The devil will come, and Faustus must be damn'd.
> Christopher Marlowe
> (1564–93)
> *Doctor Faustus*, Sc. 16

Set a beggar on horseback, and he'll outride the Devil.
> Bohn: *Foreign Proverbs, German*
> (1855)

Sarcasm I now see to be, in general, the language of
the Devil; for which reason I have, long since, as good as
renounced it.

197

Thomas Carlyle (1795–1881)
Sartor Resartus, Book II,
Chap. 4

When men grow virtuous in their old age, they
only make a sacrifice to God of the devil's leavings.
Alexander Pope (1688–1744)
Thoughts on Various Subjects

What is got over the Devil's back is spent under the
belly.
François Rabelais (1490–1553)
Works, Book V, Chap. 11

And with necessity,
The tyrant's plea, excus'd his devilish deeds.
John Milton,
Paradise Lost, Book IV,
Line 393

One dreadful sound could the Rover hear,
A sound as if with the Inchcape Bell
The Devil below was ringing his knell.
Robert Southey (1774–1843)
The Inchcape Rock, Stanza 17

He's tough, ma'am, tough, is J. B. Tough and devilish
sly.
Charles Dickens (1812–70)
Dombey and Son, Chap. 7

With devotion's visage
And pious action we do sugar o'er
The devil himself.
William Shakespeare
Hamlet, Act III, Sc. 1, Line 47

198

This wisdom descendeth not from above,
but is earthly, sensual, devilish.
James III:15

"Prophet!" said I, "thing of evil!—
prophet still, if bird or devil!"
Edgar Allan Poe (1809–49)
The Raven, Stanza 16

The saying of Molière came into his head: "But what
the devil was he doing in that galley?" and he laughed at
himself.
Leo Tolstoi
War and Peace, Part IV, Chap. 6

Why should the Devil have all the good tunes?
Rowland Hill (1744–1833)
Sermons

. . . when you have extinguished his soul in this world
and placed him where the ray of hope is blown out as in
the darkness of the damned, are you quite sure that the
demon you have roused will not turn and rend you?
Abraham Lincoln (1809–65)
Speech, Edwardsville, Illinois,
September 11, 1858

There was a Brutus once that would have brook'd
The eternal devil to keep his state in Rome
As easily as a king.
William Shakespeare
Julius Caesar, Act I, Sc. 2,
Line 158

Speak the truth and shame the Devil.
François Rabelais,

Works, Book V, Author's
Prologue

The devil can cite Scripture for his purpose.
William Shakespeare
The Merchant of Venice,
Act I, Sc. 3, Line 99

To give the devil his due.
Miguel de Cervantes,
Don Quixote, Part I,
Book III, Chap. 3

What, man! defy the Devil: consider,
he's an enemy to mankind.
William Shakespeare,
Twelfth Night, Act III, Sc. 4,
Line 109

A woman is a dish for the gods if the devil dress her
not.
William Shakespeare,
Antony and Cleopatra, Act V, Sc. 2,
Line 274

The world, the flesh, and the devil.
Book of Common Prayer,
"The Litany"

. . . 'tis the eye of childhood
That fears a painted devil.
William Shakespeare,
Macbeth, Act II, Sc. 2, Line 52

For where God built a church, there the Devil would
also build a chapel.

Martin Luther
Table Talk, 67

A savage place! as holy and enchanted
As e'er beneath a waning moon was haunted
By woman wailing for her demon-lover.

Samuel Taylor Coleridge
Kubla Khan

How then was the Devil dressed?
O, he was in his Sunday's best;
His coat was red, and his breeches were blue,
And there was a hole where his tail came through.

Robert Southey (1774–1843)
The Devil's Walk, Stanza 3

O woman, perfect woman! what distraction
Was meant to mankind when thou wast made a devil!

John Fletcher (1579–1625)
Monsieur Thomas, Act III, Sc. 1

Quit, quit, for shame, this will not move,
  This cannot take her.
If of herself she will not love,
  Nothing can make her.
  The devil take her!

Sir John Suckling (1609–42)
Song, Stanza 3

Nay, then, let the devil wear black,
for I'll have a suit of sables.

William Shakespeare,
Hamlet, Act III, Sc. 2, Line 138

Here lived the soul enchanted
  By melody of song;

Here dwelt the spirit haunted
  By a demoniac throng.
                    John Henry Boner
                    (1845–1903)
                    Poe's Cottage at Fordham

The devil take the hindmost!
                    Francis Beaumont (1584–1616)
                    and John Fletcher (1579-1625)
                    Philaster, Act V

Fifteen men on the Dead Man's Chest—
  Yo-ho-ho, and a bottle of rum!
Drink and the devil had done for the rest—
  Yo-ho-ho, and a bottle of rum!
                    Robert Louis Stevenson
                    (1850–1894)
                    Treasure Island

And neither the angels in Heaven above
  Nor the demons down under the sea,
Can ever dissever my soul from the soul
  Of the beautiful Annabel Lee.
                    Edgar Allan Poe
                    Annabel Lee, Stanza 5

Jim was most ruined for a servant, because he got
stuck up on account of having seen the devil and been
rode by witches.
                    Mark Twain,
                    Adventures of Huckleberry Finn,
                    Chap. 2

And thus I clothe my naked villainy
With odd old ends stol'n forth of holy writ,

And seem a saint when most I play the devil.
> William Shakespeare,
> *King Richard III*, Act I, Sc. 3,
> Line 336

The Devil is a gentleman.
> Percy Bysshe Shelley,
> *Peter Bell the Third*, Part II, Stanza 2

And his eyes have all the seeming of a
  demon's that is dreaming,
And the lamp-light o'er him streaming
  throws his shadow on the floor.
> Edgar Allan Poe,
> *The Raven*, Stanza 18

From his brimstone bed, at break of day,
  A-walking the Devil is gone,
To look at his little snug farm of the World,
  And see how his stock went on.
> Robert Southey,
> *The Devil's Walk*, Stanza 1

God is Love, I dare say. But what a mischievous devil
Love is.
> Samuel Butler, *Note-Books*
> *Higgledy-Piggledy:*
> *An Apology for the Devil*

O thou invisible spirit of wine! if thou
has no name to be known by, let us call thee devil!
> William Shakespeare,
> *Othello*, Act II, Sc. 3, Line 285

If two New Hampshiremen aren't a match for the

devil, we might as well give the country back to the Indians.

Stephen Vincent Benet
(1898–1943)
The Devil and Daniel Webster

Chapter Thirteen

The Devil's Adversaries

Those who perform the rites of exorcism are called exorcists; they are the principal adversaries of the devil and his agents. Historically they have had a varied career and been received with the entire gamut of human emotions. In most ages they have inspired reverence; in others they have provoked fear—but few nationalities have been brave enough to heap scorn on the heads of exorcists.

The exorcist has survived in his profession from the days of the cave dwellers to the time when man stepped on the moon. The current indications are that the exorcists are very much in style today, certainly as necessary as medical men and psychiatrists, and there is likely to be a future for anyone taking up this ancient and honored profession. A few years ago, exorcists were as hard to find as the proverbial needle in the haystack, and the fourth minor order of Roman Catholic priests was reluctant to add exorcism to its many duties. Laymen were suspect, and parapsychologists were thought fit enough to hunt ghosts but not to do battle with the devil. All that has changed, and we have an increasing number of public and private figures ready and willing to endanger their lives by declaring war on the devil and his increasing desire to possess human beings.

To date it is not possible to let your fingers "walk" through the Yellow Pages in order to track down an exorcist. The parish priest or any dedicated man of the cloth is still available for issuing "eviction orders."

"In the name of Jesus Christ of Nazareth," thunders a minister, "how many demons are you inside this boy?" The exorcist in this case was the Reverend Walter Martin, Baptist and director of the Christian Research Institute in Wayne, New Jersey. The boy was a thirteen-year-old victim of possession, and in reply to the exorcist, he said he had ten demons within him. He was violent, abusive and seemed to have the strength of at least ten demons within him. One by one, each demon was cast out until only one remained. The boy's hands clawed at his throat, as if something were trying to strangle him. "In the name of Jesus Christ of Nazareth, demon come out!" Again the Reverend Martin cried out, not this time with thunder in his voice, but almost exhausted with the strain of the exorcism. After four more hours the last demon left the boy and another nightmare was over.

In France the Reverend Henri Gesland keeps regular office hours in a subdued suite, two floors above the headquarters of the Archbishop of Paris, François Cardinal Marty. The possessed are more orderly than one would expect and line up every Wednesday morning at eight o'clock. Perhaps the antiseptic atmosphere of this modern building of the Paris Roman Catholic diocese has something to do with the unusual quietness. They are content to wait patiently for the sixty-eight-year-old Gesland, the official exorcist for this region of Paris.

He was appointed to the office in 1968 and has listened to three thousand clients, but says that only four of them could truly be cited as cases of demonic possession. Everyone gets the same treatment; the good man leaves nothing to chance. If there is no devil there, then the Litany of the Saints and the Fifty-third Psalm can only do them good anyway. If the devil is lurking in only a minor number of his clients, then Gesland is competent to deal with him. The Fifty-third Psalm is the one that describes the corruption of the wicked. Holy water is splashed on the possessed and the evil demons ordered to flee, never to return again.

In a normal day of possible contact with the devil, the Reverend Gesland sees twenty-five patients. Some wrestle with their internal anguish while others read the news sheets or magazines. But these patients are not there because they have nothing better to do. Many of them believe someone has cast a spell over them. It may be only a neighbor, but on the other hand, it could also be the devil. Gesland is a good listener and gives practical advice when the rites of full exorcism are not needed. Sometimes he suggests that the visitor see a psychiatrist and helps others simply by lending a sympathetic ear.

He has had no special training as an exorcist. After thirty years in Ceylon as a missionary, he assisted another priest in exorcising a woman who was possessed by several demons. When the exorcist in charge resigned, the diocese called on him to continue the work.

One of his most difficult cases involving true possession concerned two thirteen-year-old girls. One changed from a normal, lovable child to a hellcat who insulted her parents, relations, friends and teachers. She used obscene language and when she walked in front of lamps, the lights went out. When she sat in rooms, articles fell from their positions, although she was closely watched and witnesses stated that she never touched them. Reverend Gesland decided that exorcism was in order and did three sessions, lasting from two to three hours each.

In this case, he used the long official Latin prayer that asks who the evil spirit is and then why it is in a person. He ordered the demon to give a sign that it was prepared to leave. He continued to pray and the child, who had been rolling on the floor of the church, appeared to be more calm. It was the calm before the storm. When the priest held out the pectoral cross, she hurled it onto the floor and the convulsions started again. As she calmed down again, her parents prepared to take her away. As they left the church, the child opened her mouth and a miraculous medal fell out. The Reverend Gesland states with confidence that she could not have had access to it, much less placed it in her mouth. She recovered and the devil lost another victim.

The other girl spoke fluent Italian and German when she was possessed, although she had no knowledge of either language in her normal state. She, too, was given the full rites of exorcism and recovered.

In Florida the rector of St. Sebastian's-by-the-Sea Episcopal Church in Melbourne Beach is the Reverend Charles Stewart. In 1973 he fought demonic forces about twenty times. He talks seriously about medicine and religion and is sad that many people who could be helped by exorcism are left unaided. He also expresses the opinion that many of the beds in mental hospitals are filled with people who are possessed and therefore could benefit from exorcism. But he will not reveal his own brand of exorcism rites in case they are used by people without the necessary knowledge or appreciation of the dangers.

"I would rather hand them a box of rattlesnakes," he said. "If the rites are incomplete, the person attempting the exorcism leaves himself open to invasion by the demons." But he does have specific rules for conducting any exorcism. He never performs in public places, never in front of children or animals, since both are naturally vulnerable to the influence of Satan and his demons. He prefers to receive Holy Communion first before performing the rites and he likes to have two witnesses. One of these persons prays constantly all through the exorcism and asks for the protection of the Holy Spirit. Like many of the ancient priests, Father Stewart was himself exorcised before he began to practice himself. He does not want to be known as the exorcist of the local community, but despite this, he has gained quite a reputation in Melbourne Beach.

Some one hundred and fifty miles south of Melbourne Beach lies Miami, mecca of human snowbirds who come down for the season to escape the rigors of northern winters. Exorcism is a daily occurrence at one Miami hospital, which treats several hundred patients a month who ask to have evil spirits expelled from their bodies. Dr. Hardat Sukhdeo is the director of the Jackson Memorial Hospital, and from an average of six hundred people a month, the hospital now has more than nine hundred coming for help.

While the snowbirds only come for the season, the residential population in recent years has been augmented by a large influx of Jamaicans, Haitians, Bahamians, Cubans and Puerto Ricans. The belief that demons can infiltrate a person's body is old hat to them. They know it and also know that the possessed or seemingly possessed are entitled to help. If the devils are not at work, then an unfriendly neighbor may put a hex on any one of them and the end result is that self-confidence is lost, life seems to be on a disaster course, and mind, body and spirit are in discord. Whether it is a devil or a hex, the feeling of being damned is much the same, and fear is an emotion that breeds many types of sickness. Call it hysteria or anything else, but all these people need help and Dr. Sukhdeo, aided by his staff of thirty, sees that they get it. When a person believes he has been hexed and then it is discovered that his heart is beating 160 to the minute, he is sweating profusely and his blood pressure is low, what else can a doctor do but give help even when the patient says a fellow Jamaican has put the evil eye on him?

There is no chanting or sprinkling of powder or burning of incense. A standard fee of twelve dollars plus a lot of understanding brings the same relief as an official exorcism. Sometimes "to believe" is "to be," and whether a medical man or a priest administers help does not really matter. Of course there are going to be many more cases of pseudo-possession, and this is going to be one of the problems of the future. The important thing is to have enough people able to recognize each for what it is and then to act according to the needs.

Not only are members of the religious world split in their acceptance of the credibility of demon possession and exorcism, but there is more than a little controversy about the idea that the devil is rampaging around the world, working *on* people if not always *in* them. Temptation, obsession and possession are three manifestations of his work. In Hawaii, as full of little people as Ireland, the Reverend Fred Cordeiro of Ewa Beach claims to have performed 115 exorcisms in the past five years. He is the fundamentalist minister of the Ewa Beach Assembly of God church and did his first exorcism in 1969. He says he has seen people slither like snakes, others claw at themselves, and still others, like bears, display amazing strength. He has had many cases in which obscene language has given way to speaking in tongues. Welts, lacerations, and the marks of huge teeth have appeared on the bodies of some victims of possession. Like all good exorcists, Reverend Cordeiro is not afraid. He says, "As long as I am protected by the blood of the Lord, nothing will hurt me. I stand in power and authority of God, and demons tremble. A spirit must be commanded out of the body. I fire questions at it until it manifests itself through the individual's tongue. Then I bind it in the name of the Lord." An exorcism can take many hours, but Cordeiro is not a man who will give up, although demons have sometimes threatened to kill him. The Reverend Cordeiro always gets his demons.

Despite the impression given by James Michener's remarkable book on Hawaii, the royal priest cult of the Kuhanas is as strong as ever today. The Kuhanas have their own inimitable way of dealing with the possessed, although few will discuss it. In recent years I have become friendly with many Kuhanas, both male and female, and they freely admit that Dr. Cordeiro's numerically impressive exorcisms are not representative of the total number of exorcisms that have actually taken place on the island. When in any type of trouble, the native Hawaiian is more likely to go to the Kuhana than to anyone else; even if he prays in church, he knows that the Kuhanas have a particularly strong type of psychic medicine. In tune with all the spirits of nature, they recognize evil and are well equipped to expel it with incantations, authority and herbs. Probably the last remnants of the great psychic healers in the world, the Kuhanas recognize that an evil spirit can cause sickness, and destroy the mind and body. All forms of exorcism are really spiritualized means of healing, so that the mind, body and spirit will come into harmony again.

In Italy Monseigneur Luigi Novarese is very much on the spot for performing exorcisms. He has done this work for twenty-five years and sees Satan as a real and totally terrifying figure but has never been afraid to go into hundreds of battles with him. Monseigneur Novarese fulfills the Roman Catholic church's requirements for the work of driving out devils: he is a man of wide experience and high morality. To those engaged in this work, the devil is never treated lightly. He is no playmate, no figment of the imagination, but the most evil of all spirits, whose sole purpose is to exploit man and literally get him by any means possible—and the quickest route to success is through possession. The priests know their enemy and treat the devil as such.

Another modern exorcist in Rome is Father Gabriel

of the order of the Servants of Mary in the Roman Church of the Seven Founder Saints. People come from all over the world to visit him and use his services, and he has a reputation for being very successful. Both priests admit that today they are feeling the strain and understand that the released demons often try to take revenge on the exorcist. They are strong and through their staunehly held beliefs so far can resist the temptations and torment of the devil.

One good thing about the new awareness of the devil and his work is that the responsibility and strain of exorcism is now being more equally distributed. Until a few years ago, most of the Roman Catholic priests I knew were elderly, but many more of the younger priests are anxious to come to grips with driving out the devils. Permission to do so must always come from a higher authority, and I believe there is an increased interest in training the young priests who are fearless enough to want to use the rites of exorcism. The entire rite is virtually a cleansing process as well as therapeutic, inasmuch as it is designed to heal the possessed person in body and soul.

In New York City, at St. Bonaventure University, a priest who teaches theology has also had some experience in exorcism. He is the Reverend Alphonse Trabold, an earnest, bespectacled young man who, of course, maintains his belief in the traditional teaching of the Roman Catholic church that Satan is a personal being, the angel who turned against God. He admits that science has gone a long way in helping civilized man with fears of the devil and his legion. While some of the phenomena once attributed to possession can be cleared up by proper medical treatment, such an explanation does not rule out the fact that the devil has an influence on earth.

When all other treatments have failed and the phenomenon persists, then exorcism is justified and should be performed. Sometimes the priest performs the lengthy regular religious rite of exorcism, but it is more usual to talk to victims and try to implant the love of God within them and make them aware of his compassion. I think the Reverend Trabold expresses the views of many of the younger priests, but there may be some danger in attempting to modify the old and well-tested official type of exorcism. I am confident that each priest faced with a case of possession will always do his best, and many priests are also trained in psychology; but it is in the realms of spirituality where they are likely to be most effective. Relations and those close to a possessed person still have faith in religious rites in times of dire emergency, and what could constitute an emergency so much as a case of possession?

Each to his own, and while parapsychologists, laymen, shamans and witches are also capable of exorcism, the function of the priest in holy orders is to work within the framework of what he knows and understands best, and hopefully that is his own religion and its canon laws. Protection can be taken by those who are near to a possessed person, and again this is also within the framework of his specific beliefs. The Star of David has deep, esoteric meaning for a Jew, the crucifix or medallions of the saints for a Catholic; the Protestant has his cross, prayer book and Bible. The less orthodox religions, valid to those who follow them, can be protected by waving a pentagram, one of the most ancient symbols of protection. Whatever we have a deep faith in ultimately becomes imbued with special protective forces, and a sincere belief in the efficacy of charms, talismans and amulets serves to reinforce what should be a deep inner conviction that good must always overcome evil. Most of all, there should be a total acceptance that any evil spirit can be commanded to leave the body of the possessed in the name of the highest deity within the comprehension of the exorcist.

One of the greatest dangers of the present time is that many people, motivated by the desire to help, may try to improvise forms of exorcism. This do-it-yourself exorcism is fraught with dangers, and the well-meaning friend is no substitute for a professional exorcist. The danger becomes twofold, since the possessed may get worse and the amateur, himself, become infected. If this happens on a large scale, we can expect epidemics of possession spreading as rapidly as measles once did in a kindergarten. Inexperienced exorcists can themselves present as much of a problem as anyone who thinks that surgery can be performed on the kitchen table with the aid of a vegetable knife. True, those who are inclined toward do-it-yourself exorcisms are often ill-informed about the seriousness of possession and the hazards of the task. Others, however, may find exorcism a means of boosting their own egos, and perhaps it is among these people that the greatest danger lies.

It is necessary to know the entire case history of a possessed person, just as a doctor should know the case history of anyone coming to him for treatment. First of all, it is no use taking it for granted that a person says he is possessed. In genuine cases the last person to be concerned about exorcism is the possessed, since he is in the grip of the devil, who is very happy to remain within the body. So the majority of cases are brought to light by those in close contact with the stricken person, and they begin to look around for help.

I am not sure if there is, indeed, a stigma attached to being possessed, although in ultra-Puritanic circles this may well be the case. We all know that even today we are not yet enlightened enough to face even a case of mental illness without some sense of guilt and the desire to keep such an illness a secret. This is illogical, but unfortunately it is true, despite constant propaganda put out by committees studying mental illness. It can only be hoped that anyone who thinks he may have a relation or friend who is possessed will at least not be afraid to look for help; it is important to get the best available help.

No one should charge for exorcism, something that is likely to happen when a layman is approached to perform the act. Gifts of love and appreciation are a different matter; I know very few people who have experienced official rites through a priest who have not desired to make a monetary contribution to the local church. I live in dread of seeing a spate of advertisements, especially in the United States, offering the service of exorcism for a specific number of dollars. I firmly believe that most laborers are worthy of their hire, but the thought of charging a fee and cashing in on the most abject form of misery known to man revolts me. Curiosity about psychic phenomena often results in a careless approach to the subject such as when people play at having a séance "just for the fun of it" without realizing that they are dealing with forces stronger than themselves. The good intentions of the average person who thinks he knows something about psychic phenomena are not enough. There are times when an expert is needed and in this case it is the exorcist and it is pertinent to remember that a little knowledge can be dangerous. Worse still is the thought that exorcism should be given the three ring circus treatment with friends invited in to witness the victim in his agony and the exorcist performing. Life at all levels is very public today with the media of television and radio always looking for fresh subjects to intrigue the viewers and listeners. Already the attention of many a producer is turned towards making a public spectacle of exorcism. If this ever happens, it will not only make things worse for the possessed but it will also set up a foundation for the devil to create further confusion. Possession is as contagious as typhoid fever or the measles.

Possession is an emotional state, and emotion is felt by the exorcist, although at no time should he try to relate to the demon or the possessed. So while he must surely feel several emotions, such as compassion, he must never become emotionally involved; otherwise he becomes more vulnerable to the wiles of the devil.

In most cases the possessed will try to sidetrack the exorcist, sometimes by abuse, often by flattery and cajolery, in fact anything that will cause a break in the rhythm of words. When this fails, the possessed generally follows a pattern of excessive violence, also designed to break the regular flow of the exorcism. The exorcist knows that the demons have a vast repertoire of actions designed to disrupt his work. It is not easy to pray and incant when slime is spewed into the room and on the body of the exorcist. Changes of temperature, icy winds and sudden noises of a terrifying nature are

217

thrown in as well. This is why most exorcisms do not succeed at once and take several days or weeks to bring about results.

Imagine a priest going to his first exorcism; he may have heard stories about other exorcisms, but nothing is quite as bad as the actual confrontation with evil manifesting itself in a dozen different ways. Most human beings react violently to seweragelike smells that cause retching. Supernatural acts, such as the body of the possessed rising in the air or causing furniture to move around, and lurid welts appearing on the body are enough to make strong men feel weak and inadequate . . . which is exactly what the demons want to happen. I would say that most exorcists have to go through the entire performance of tricks at least once before they can settle down and be sufficiently confident to carry on no matter what happens.

The yardstick of success is measured by the exorcist's belief in his own powers; his ability to succeed will rest on the intensity of his own beliefs. No matter how many times the exorcist is thrown off guard, he must always go back and complete the job he started. If he does not, then as likely as not he, too, becomes possessed. For exorcism is a battle to the death. The devil is not likely to die, but the exorcist faces the danger of personal injury.

At some point in the exorcism the possessed will recognize that someone is trying to help. It may be only a momentary flash, but the exorcist must seize on it and try to strengthen the bond, fragile though it may be. The recognition may come in the form of a weakly spoken word, almost lost in the avalanche of cursing that always follows. Or it may be through the eyes when for a tiny second the bestial, inhuman look is replaced by one of a human being pleading for help. It is essential for the exorcist to understand that he is dealing with the remnants of a human being, an entity in itself and the separate entity or entities of the invading forces. The demons will struggle all the time for domination and even acceptance by the exorcist, and it is this force that must be broken.

The devil or his demons will play game after game, always trying to attract attention. With the ability to make predictions, some are sure to be startling enough to excite interest. If that is not enough, then the demons will try to throw in a sudden revelation about something in the past of the exorcist. Generally this is some little-known point that the exorcist knows cannot be common knowledge. Strong nerves have to go with strong faith, and at any hint of fear or hesitation the demons rollick around in the possessed. Any tiny sense of insecurity is readily picked up by them and taken advantage of. Since tremendous energy is within the power of the demons, they are likely to be able to continue their antics for twenty-four hours without rest. Exorcism becomes a rite of endurance, a marathon of spiritual energy, and always an awareness of the material side as well. Expletives are intangible but full of foul vibrations that can pierce the psyche like arrows; the activities may include throwing around objects with the exorcist as the target.

The church has always differentiated between solemn and simple exorcism. The former is undertaken only by priests; the latter can be performed by others. Whether priest or layman, the conflict between the demons and the exorcist is guaranteed to be fearful and nerve-wracking. The priest has some advantages over the layman, inasmuch as he should be well prepared by virtue of his everyday life. Many laymen, however, lead exemplary lives and know that preparation before undertaking an exorcism is important, whether the preparation is by prayers or meditation; it should be done with dedication and an enormous sense of faith that the deity will help.

Both solemn and simple exorcism can be effective, but the layman rarely sits in judgment of the possessed once he has been cleansed. The priest will always believe it his duty to encourage the once-possessed to accept baptism in his church as a means of fending off any future attacks. I use the word "priest" to include clergymen of the Protestant faiths as well. Roman Catholics are concerned with the full conversion of the once-possessed, Protestants that the victim renew his baptismal vows. Renunciation of evil is the object for priests and other clergymen, but the latter have a less complicated method of renunciation, based on the Decision in the New Baptism Service of 1967, which simply states three vows:

1. I turn to Christ.
2. I repent of my sins.
3. I renounce evil.

The blocking of the memory is generally a means of salvation to the victim of possession, and this block is reinforced by relations, friends and clergymen or priests. Constant questioning after the exorcism is dangerous because it may lead to some memories returning, and the danger of new guilt complexes becomes evident. Deliverance does not actually end with the expulsion of the demon, and gentle compassion and tolerance may be the final attributes needed to complete the healing of the inharmonious mind, body and spirit. Healing and deliverance are among the lost arts of many religious groups, and in many cases have to be effected by staunch friends and laymen who become the new age's good Samaritans.

The work of the exorcist is tremendously difficult. Rewards come not through the ego but through the appreciation that such work has saved the life and reason of another human being. With real spirituality within the exorcists, this is enough.

Chapter Fourteen

The Psyche – the Achilles' Heel of Man

Among the most popular news stories today are reports of numerous cases of exorcism. Exorcists all over the world lay claim to having exorcised vast numbers of demons. The Reverend Christopher Neil Smith of England claims to have performed more than two thousand exorcisms since 1969, and there is no reason to doubt the number of cases. What is in doubt is that the devil or any of his demons were the cause of the possession in every case. I believe that many cases today are the result of psychic attacks, with perhaps ten percent of the total coming within the province of the devil.

In the first two chapters of this book I described how the Leek family was possessed. But the possession was by psychic attack, which can be just as evil and awe-inspiring as possession by the devil. Mediums are often subjected to such attacks, and it is not a figment of the imagination that the man in the street can be hexed, cursed or suffer the malignant effects of black magic. No matter what may be the cause of possession, the right approach is through exorcism and that means the expulsion of the entity temporarily occupying the human body. Highly psychic people who are not trained and may not know they are psychic can enter certain rooms or be in a specific place and pick up the vibrations of an earthbound spirit unable to go to another place to be reincarnated. The professional medium goes to investigate a haunting, knowing that he may be possessed by one of the entities causing the disturbance. He is able to free himself from the entity either by his own efforts or through the help of a parapsychologist. Only an emergency should allow any medium to work on his own; it is always better to have someone else around. Just as two detectives often go together to interrogate a suspect, mediums should work in pairs.

The man in the street exposed to psychic attacks can become sick, function in a totally different way from the way he usually does, go to the doctor and be told that nothing is wrong with him, or begin to think that he is going mad. He may go through all these phases before he goes to a medium, priest or clergyman to be exorcised.

One of the major attributes of the present occult explosion is that more and more people are aware that psychic attacks, hexes and black magic are real. An awareness that psychic phenomena are no longer to be considered nonsense helps people get themselves sorted out by whatever means are available. Remember that people of all faiths are possible candidates for psychic attacks.

It is unfortunate that few priests and clergymen are willing to help, so the unfortunate victim goes to a medium or even a witch who may also have mediumistic qualities. The battle to release the victim from the entity can be just as difficult as in the more dramatic case when the devil or his demons have taken over a human body. The physical phenomena may not be so drastic in cases of psychic attack. For instance, there are not so many welts on the body, not so much grotesqueness and never the declaration that the body is inhabited by the devil himself.

The exorcist must always try to get the entity to name itself, and there is a sigh of genuine relief when an entity declares itself to be, say, the incarnate spirit of Sarah Marshall, who died in 1750. Sarah may have been a murderess or a less-than-likable person, but there is a big difference between Sarah and the devil himself. Sarah does not want to possess the soul of the human being and take it to hell; she just wants her moment on earth again, either to give a message or simply to savor the feeling of being in the world again. Distressed spirits can be very evil, mischievous—or possibly even benevolent—and are the main cause of what we call ghost phenomena, but there is a psychotic quality about the ghost, a spirit lost in time and place. The fact is that no human body needs to share itself with a discarnate spirit for any length of time. It is better to expel it and send it to another dimension, where it can await reincarnation.

Many types of psychic attack are able to work through the principles of telepathic suggestion of three kinds: autosuggestion, conscious suggestion, and hypnotic suggestion. All make their mark on the conscious mind. The voodoo artist and the black magician know how to project strong forces by directing the power of thought toward the chosen target. By the reiteration of incantations and total concentration on the victim, the vibrations from one mind go out on the ether and reach their target. It is a classic example of mind over matter, and the evil thoughts begin to manifest themselves on the victim in any number of ways: wasting of the body tissues for no apparent medical cause, changes in personality and, in extreme cases, death.

The medium going to investigate a haunted house uses autosuggestion to place herself in a position whereby the entities causing the disturbance can use her body and vocal cords to express themselves. Once this is done, the entities are glad to go of their own volition. If they persist in trying to remain, they are expelled by a simple exorcism given by the parapsychologist. Conscious suggestion is generally used as an extension of autosuggestion, but not necessarily as a means of contacting spirits. It is more likely to be used to try to expel a personal fear. Unfortunately with the preponderance of many correspondence courses on conscious suggestion, a form of personal hypnotism, the untrained person leaves areas of his psyche wide open for another entity to creep in. Rarely is this a good entity; more often than not it is a mischievous or even demonlike creature in a low state of spiritual evolution. Just as children can play havoc in an empty house by smashing windows, so these entities can play havoc with the human being.

Hypnotic suggestion enters the subconscious mind directly without impinging on the consciousness at all. Hypnotic suggestion literally means suggestion during sleep. It can be achieved through the services of a hypnotist, and also by a voodoo practitioner or a black magician. In the latter case direct contact with the victim need not occur, and this is where the most mischief can be achieved. Suggestions made in this way are rarely recognized as coming from an outside force and are only discovered after they have grown and taken hold of the subconscious. It is an invisible seed, which grows rapidly until the entire personality of the victim is taken over, literally possessed by whatever demonic qualities the black magician or voodoo practitioner had in mind. For certain, the practitioners are not concerned with general well-being of the chosen subject but are directed to nullify the normal instincts of the victims and, in some dire cases, achieve the death of the subject.

Such psychic attacks have been the mainstay of science fiction and Gothic horror writers for a long time. Today the horror is in the fact that what once seemed to be fiction is now something stranger than truth. Cases of possession by psychic attack are due to the vicious motivations of the practitioner sending the attacks. He may well be a servant of the devil and generally is at least dedicated to pursuing evil, so the overall effects turn out to be evil.

There are examples of some cases of psychic possession, however, that are beneficial (although evil cases seem to dominate the scene). For instance, Mrs. Rosemary Brown, who has made psychic-phenomena history by being able to write music through possession of her mind by famous dead composers, has experienced the most benevolent type of possession.

Many people throughout the world are today knowledgeable about the numerous possessions that have overtaken me, since these have been widely written about by Professor Hans Holzer and other parapsychologists. Less widely known are my own determined efforts to free people who are under psychic attack, and

226

in some cases I have had my personal confrontation with demons. Like other exorcists, my cases of releasing victims from psychic attack greatly outnumber the confrontations with demons.

One such case, however, stands out in my mind. Several years ago I had a phone call from a well-known editor of a publishing house in New York City. I had done a book for him, but at the time I was not under contract to the house. However I had become very friendly with the editor, on a social basis and through mutual friends in the literary world. I was surprised to receive his phone call because he seemed very disturbed and was obviously beating about the bush before coming to the reason for his phone call. He told me he had a friend he had known for something like twenty years. He gave me the background history of his friend, who for many years had been an executive of the famous advertising company of J. Walter Thompson. The editor emphasized that his friend had been a highly responsible individual, well respected in his business and earning a considerable amount of money. He named some of the story boards his friend had been responsible for and advertising campaigns he had devised. The list was impressive, and I could hardly wait to hear the real reason for the phone call.

The editor explained that his friend had changed within the past six months. His personality was entirely different; he was aggressive and violent. His work suffered and he was given sick leave, which he spent going from one doctor to another and then from one psychiatrist to yet another psychiatrist. He thought he must be going mad and had reached a stage when he was quite prepared to enter a mental institution. The trouble was, no one would take him in. He went for one interview and the medical man wondered why he was there.

I asked the editor if there was any noticeable loss of weight in his friend, and he said there was, and that the man had always enjoyed active participation in sports, that he was six feet tall and weighed two hundred pounds. In the last six months he had lost sixty pounds, hated exercise of any kind and was living like an animal. The editor had visited him in his elegant apartment on the East Side of New York and found it a shambles, filthy and full of disgusting smells. He also spoke of horrible eating mannerisms and a depraved appetite, even to the point of asking for substances that are never considered as food. Remember that for numerous years, he was known for his sybaritic lifestyle, his good manners, and general appreciation of the finer things of life. It was because of the visit to the apartment that the editor finally called me.

I asked him what he wanted me to do and he suggested that I see the man. When I asked why, he hesitated and then blurted out, "Sybil, you will never believe this . . . but . . . I think he is possessed!" I made no comment but said I would see him. The difficulty was how to arrange it. My friendly concerned editor said he would purchase an airplane ticket and send him down to Florida to see me. "He knows who you are," he said, "so I think he will come."

Somewhat reluctantly I agreed that this would be all right, and we left it that he would call me again and tell me when to expect his friend. We had a phone call and my two sons went to the local airport to pick him up. I suggested they call me as soon as he arrived and give me their opinion.

It is barely possible to come to Melbourne Beach from New York and return the same day, so I was faced with wondering what to do with the man. I did not like the idea of having a strange male in the house, but neither did I like to send him to a motel. After all, Melbourne Beach is a very small place and every motel keeper knows me, so anyone sent to them by me could produce repercussions if anything went wrong. I had a dismayed feeling about how wrong things could be and was agreeably surprised when Stephen called me to say that the man had arrived. He said he looked very ill but was soft spoken and had carried on a pleasant conversation. The main emphasis was that he looked frightfully ill and seemed very weak, so much so that the overnight bag he carried was almost too much for him to handle.

Quickly I booked a room at a nearby motel, but asked them to bring him straight to my house on Riverside Drive. I watched them from a window as they decanted themselves from the car. I saw a tall, emaciated man, dark-haired and well-dressed but with eyes I can only describe as haunted. I could also see that at one time he must have been very good-looking

I had prepared English-style tea with cookies and small sandwiches to be served in the living room, pleasantly placed facing the river where we could see the sunshine. The house was serene and beautiful, and if it were only a malaise he was suffering, he must surely respond to the peacefulness of the environment.

I opened the front door and introductions were effected in stilted formality. We all sat down to partake

229

of the food and tea. I noticed that our visitor refused to eat anything but literally grabbed a cup of tea in a pleasing English porcelain vessel. He grabbed it with both hands and literally poured it down his throat instead of drinking it.

When we had greeted each other, his voice had been quietly modulated and showed the signs of a good education—or at least some trace of elocution. When he had swallowed the tea, with accompanying disgusting noises, which we all tried to ignore, he shoved the cup toward me and in a deep, animal cry said: *"More!"* I poured him another cup and he threw it down his throat. I marveled that he could drink it so hot because I left it to him to add sugar, cream or lemon as he wished, but he took it plain.

After a short silence he sat back in his chair, studying us all from half-closed eyes. I thought we had better keep the conversation going. We talked about Florida and New York; he replied in what I presumed was his normal voice, quite gently and relaxed. The boys left, pausing at the door to ask if they should let the cats out. Whenever I have a visitor for the first time in my house, I always keep the cats in another part of the house, since everyone is not as fond of pets as I am. When I told the boys to leave the cats where they were, our visitor opened his eyes and remarked that he was very fond of animals. I noticed that his eyes looked quite vacant, although the voice had a charismatic quality.

I told him I had booked a room for him at the motel but would like him to stay to dinner. He did not seem interested in the idea but said he wanted to talk. Well, that was half the reason he had come, so we put off dinner, walked around the pool and then settled into the living room. In the course of the evening, he told me he was once married to a South American girl but had been divorced for three years. I did not question him about the marriage or the divorce, but went on to talk about South America and to say that I had always been interested in that area of the world and had numerous relations scattered about.

"Even hear of the Umbanda cult?" he asked.

Indeed, I had heard of it and had talked to many people belonging to the cult. The rituals are an extreme type of advanced voodooism. At meetings members allow themselves to be possessed, but it is a hit-and-miss case whether the possession is by a good or evil spirit. The ultimate possession is by the devil, whom the Umbandas call Exu. I had no intention of telling my new friend how much I knew.

"Well, at least you know something about South America and that there is a strong, faithful following of the Umbanda." I nodded and he went on. "My ex-wife belonged to the cult. When we visited her country several times, she would go off and come back tremendously exhilarated. It was as if everything she wanted, she got."

I could imagine why, but kept silent.

"I didn't like it and made the mistake of saying so. She was angry, but because I loved her, I agreed to go to a meeting. Not with the intention of taking part in anything; just to be with her."

It seems that he went to the meeting and was appalled by what he saw and begged his wife never to go again. On returning to New York he started to have nightmares. His wife laughed and told him that they would continue until he became more agreeable to the

231

I felt it was time for him to try to get some rest, and Julian drove him to the motel. I gave him some advice about trying to relax and also a piece of jewelry I was accustomed to wearing.

"Please," I begged him, "if you feel any strange sensation coming over you, just focus your eyes on this. Wear it if you can, but hold it in your hands if you feel strange. See, the chain is long enough. The boys will pick you up in the morning—say, nine o'clock—and bring you back here."

He thanked me and we walked down the garden path together. As he was about to get into the car, he turned his ghostlike eyes toward me, grabbed both my hands and muttered, "Help me! Help me!"

That night I did not attempt to sleep but kept my mind on the man, visualizing him in his motel room and finally visualizing him asleep. Only then could I, myself, relax—but not in sleep, merely in deep thought.

By morning I knew the only thing that could save him was an exorcism. The boys fetched him from the motel as arranged, and I began to talk to him. He interrupted to say he had had a good night's sleep and felt very good. He returned my amulet to me and I put it around my neck.

I explained about the exorcism, and he agreed to it. I had visions of taking him into my office, settling him down comfortably and then authoritatively and calmly going through the rites of exorcism. Before I could suggest this, two of my four cats rushed into the living room and pulled up sharply at the sight of the visitor, hackles rising, tails fluffed out, spitting as cats do when faced with an enemy. Before I could chide them, our

232

visitor had leaped forward and seized one of the cats and was trying to throttle her! Guismo, the old male cat, threw himself on him and clawed at his hands. Geisha got free.

Quickly I shut the door and then saw what had happened to my guest. He was a changed being, growling like an animal, then speaking a language I could not understand. He walked to one of my batiks and tore it from the wall. It was a copy of the page in the Book of Kells representing John the Baptist. He was trampling it underfoot, but I was not really concerned about that. I knew there was no time to settle him down for exorcism in the other room; it had to be done now. I began to shout the adjuration to the Mother Goddess, and he pulled up sharply, and started to rush at me but I continued with the adjuration. He fell to the floor writhing, clutching his stomach. Then he lay fairly still.

"What devil is in you?" I asked.

A loud snarling filled the room, and the drapes ballooned out as if caught in a high wind. The air conditioning was on, so no windows were open. I felt a huge gust of wind hit me in the face; the floor trembled as if there were an earthquake, and I had difficulty in standing.

"Who are you? Name yourself!" I persisted. More grunts and animal noises erupted from him, and the brass guard around the fireplace was ripped apart.

"Who are you? Tell me your name!"

A very quiet, gentle, definitely female voice said, "You are Sybil."

Well, I knew who I was, but I was not sure now who I had with me, so I went on with the adjuration, then the

Umbanda. Although he had not been a regular churchgoer, he decided to go to church. Every time he did so, he returned home to find some manifestation of psychic phenomena confronting him. One day his camera lifted itself off the shelf and hit him across the head; another time, intending to have a cold shower, he had been covered with scalding water before his hand touched the faucet.

His relationship with his wife was good, except on one subject. Whenever he tried to discuss the Umbanda, she turned on him. He began to feel very ill, but his doctor said there was nothing wrong with him. When his vacation came due, his wife had arranged for them to go to South America again. Reluctantly he went, feeling that he should be with her; in fact, he stated that he felt compelled to be with her.

"One part of me did not want to go," he said, "but another part of me insisted that I go. It seemed I had no will to oppose it." After a pleasant few days, his wife announced that she was going to the meeting of the cult and that he must go with her. Again he could not express a negative desire and went with her, athough he took with him a tiny camera. I knew from my editor friend that this man had quite a reputation as a cameraman.

He remembers going to the meeting, has a recollection of taking three photos with the miniature camera, and then remembers nothing else. He woke up in his own room at the hotel with his wife beside him. Life was never the same again; his health deteriorated, and his world fell apart. He had the film developed, though, in New York and he showed the pictures to me.

Unmistakably the three photos were of a voodoo ceremony. One was rather blurred but the other two were pretty clear. I still have the photos and, indeed, they were the clincher in my deciding to help him.

In order to escape from his wife, a divorce was arranged and to his surprise she took it very easily, even taking a malicious delight in taunting him that it was the last thing he would ever be able to do. Alone in his apartment, he had difficulties on many days in going to work and still more difficulty in concentrating on his demanding job. Finally he asked for sick leave and got it. That was when he started the rounds of doctors and psychiatrists.

"I think I was hypnotized and possessed," he said very simply. "I have gaps in my life that I cannot account for. I think I do something dreadful in this time gap. I find things I know have been stolen, in my apartment, and the place stinks as if a skunk is loose in it at times. Friends used to visit me, but then they seemed to hate the place, except for D. [my editor]. Everyone would complain about strange noises, and some asked if I had an animal in the bedroom because conversations were interspersed with whining and the sound of claws or furniture being moved around."

He paused for a minute, but I did not need him to tell me he did not have a pet of any kind.

"D. came around, and he knows I am speaking the truth; there was a black cloud in the apartment and a horrible smell. So much of the place had been smashed up by some unseen force that there was hardly a thing left whole in it. That's when D. asked me to come and see you."

questions, adjuration again, then more questions.

"In the name of Diana, the Mother Goddess," I thundered, *"Tell me your name!"*

His face was now the personification of all that is evil—lips thickened, eyes brutalized, nose swollen and running with pus. This time the voice came out of the creature and thundered its reply to me.

"I am Exu. . . ." Fiendish laughter, hitting my ears like a sonic boom, whirled around me.

But I continued with my incantation.

"Spirit of the Universe, conjure it; Spirit of the Universe, conjure it!

"Spirit of Diana, Mother of all the Universe, conjure it!

"Spirit of the watchers of the night, conjure it!

"Spirit of Brigit, conjure it!

"Spirit of Astarte, conjure it!

"Spirit of all that is good, conjure it!

"Great Mother Goddess, lady of harmony, conjure it!

"Great Earth Mother, drive out this devil!"

The creature writhed on the floor, clawing at the carpet, sightless eyes burning as if there were flames behind them.

"Leave this body, Exu!" I shouted again and again with all the firmness I could muster. "Leave this body and return to those who sent you."

"I am *Exu!*" came back the reply. Each word was spat out of the thick, blood-streaked lips.

"There is no place for you here," I said. "I am stronger than you, and I tell you to go."

"What will you give me if I go?" And now the voice was sweetly seductive, totally different from the harsh, inhuman one before.

"I do not trade with the devil," I said and said the conjuration again. I could see the creature slithering over the floor toward me, but I did not dare move. When within a yard of my foot, it stopped.

"Depart, evil Exu, and return to the one who sent you!" I yelled.

The creature laughed.

"What will you give me if I go away?"

"No bargaining," I replied. "I know you for what you are."

Back to the adjuration, again and again. Occasionally the creature snorted so that pus flew from his nostrils almost hitting my foot before landing on the carpet.

"Give me a sign that you will leave," I said.

The thing raised itself almost from the ground and emitted a foul smell that nauseated me for moment.

"In the name of Diana, the Mother Goddess, depart!"

In the hall I could hear my two parrots screaming. The screams got louder and louder, and the creature on the floor joined in. Now I knew I had him; this was the sign I had asked for. I knew from past experience, though, that this was no time to feel any flow of satisfaction. The devil is a trickster and this could be one of his tricks. Nothing for it but to continue with incantations and authoritative commands to depart.

There was a rush of wind through the room, the already fallen fire guard whirled through the air. The sonic sounds boomed again in my ears, and then there was a merciful silence. I looked at the creature on the floor. His face was normal, but rather suffused with more color than I had seen in him when he arrived. The writhing and clawing had stopped. Never had the sound of silence been so appreciated as at that moment.

The birds in the hall began to chirp and chatter to each other.

My visitor raised himself from the floor and gazed at me. I noticed his eyes seemed normal again. He did not seem to notice the mess in the room and I quickly guided him through the dining room into the library. As he eased himself into a chair, he remarked that he felt very tired, as if a bulldozer had run over him. He asked if I minded if he slept for a while. I felt like joining him, but knew better than to relax from now on. From time to time I looked in on him and he was sleeping soundly. Several hours later he awoke and we made plans to put him on a plane to New York in the late afternoon.

For several weeks afterward I had delightful letters from him; there was no mention of his ailment or what had happened.

I spoke to my editor but did not go into any gruesome details. He said whatever had happened must have done some good for his friend was looking good and had called him to say he was going to the ballet that night. It seemed a good sign that normality had returned. I could not resist a snippy remark to my editor.

"You have some nice friends, I must say, but I wish you would keep them in New York. I came to Florida for peace and quietness."

He laughed and hung up.

The case of Rose-Marie, the niece of a well-known, much-publicized member of the Mafia, was very different from the expulsion of Exu. Having spent many years in Italy and Sicily in my youth, I had made many friends in that part of the world. When my two

THE PSYCHE—THE ACHILLES' HEEL OF MAN

sons were babies, they were in danger of being totally spoiled by adoring grandmothers in Sicily. I was always exhorted to get in touch with a son, nephew, uncle or grandson, because everyone I knew in Sicily seemed to have relations in the United States. I always promised I would convey messages, but the opportunity to come to the United States did not appear for some time. I had no idea that one of my favorite families in Sicily was related to one especially famous family in America. At the annual song festival in San Remon, I met a charming, beautiful Italian girl, who had recently married one of the foremost composers in Italy. We discovered we had mutual acquaintances in Sicily, and through frequent correspondence I learned that Rose-Marie was going to live in New York, but minus her husband.

"Call me as soon as you arrive in New York," she wrote.

Well, I arrived and called her, and we happily renewed our Riviera friendship. She was beautiful, talented, and money never seemed to be a problem. We dined and lunched in some of the best Italian restaurants in New York. I traveled extensively all over the country on lecture and promotion tours.

Then I decided to spend half the year in Hollywood, California, and the other half in New York City. While in Hollywood, I had a phone call from Arizona from a man who said he was the uncle of Rose-Marie. He asked me to go to her in New York and said he feared she was in great trouble. I could not find out what the trouble was; phone calls to her luxuriously appointed Upper East Side apartment elicited nothing. The housekeeper always answered the phone, speaking almost in a whisper, and one day she called me and asked me to come to New York. Meanwhile, a plane ticket arrived for me from the uncle in Arizona, with two hundred dollar bills in an envelope, but no letter.

Obviously I was meant to follow up on this and go to New York. I caught a plane and called the apartment from Kennedy airport. Again the housekeeper answered, telling me not to go to a hotel but to go straight to the apartment.

When I reached the apartment, the housekeeper let me in and the sad story unfolded. Rose-Marie was, indeed, sick, was no longer beautiful, and her personality had changed. The best of medical attention and psychiatric care had been provided by the uncle, but nothing seemed to work. The housekeeper was Italian, elderly and quite used to the idea that magic works. I was amused at the fear and respect she accorded me, but I had lived long enough in Italy and Sicily to understand it. Both countries understand La Strega, and to them I was always to be La Strega—the witch.

I asked where Rose-Marie was. The housekeeper said she was in her room; she was afraid to go in there because strange things happened. I asked her why she stayed, because she was obviously frightened to death. "I have to stay," she said. "First the uncle tells me to and I must also look after the boy." Rose-Marie had a son, ten years old, fathered by the Italian musician. I glanced around the apartment and decided that whoever was now looking after her, was certainly doing it in great style. The housekeeper understood my inquiring gaze.

"Her uncle gives her everything, for the sake of the

family," she said. She pulled me into a room and it was a full-size dressing room. "Look!" She revealed dresses, fur coats, handbags with matching shoes, all of the finest quality and mostly made in Italy. "Everything she wants is hers."

Then she drew me quietly toward the bedroom. In the big room, elegant enough for any Hollywood house, a small figure lay in the large king-size bed. I tiptoed quietly toward the bed. Rose-Marie was not asleep but was lying there inert and lifeless, like a doll that had been dropped; her head lolled on one side and her eyes gazed at me without recognition. The room was icy cold. I noticed several broken pieces of china and winced to recognize some of it as antique Sevres.

"Did she do this?" I asked.

The housekeeper shushed me with her finger to her lips and silently we went back into the living room.

"Many things in the house are smashed," she said. "At first I thought she was doing it in a rage, but things get smashed when she is not in the room. Miss Sybil, she is possessed!"

Well, for sure something had happened to the vibrant, beautiful, young Italian girl I had known so well. She had always been the life and soul of any party, a great athletic figure on the tennis courts, capable of dancing all night, an intelligent, graceful girl, full of the joy of life. Not even the separation from her husband had upset her; we had frequently spoken about it and she regarded the separation as necessary for the time being so that she had time to think and try to understand the situation. Divorce was out of the question because of her Roman Catholic upbringing. I

241

also knew that her family was connected with the Mafia and that her uncle, having lost a private war in New York, had gone to live in Arizona.

"How long has she been like this?" I asked, marveling at the faithfulness of the housekeeper and knowing that any other domestic would have left as soon as anything unpleasant happened.

"For three months; every day she gets worse," was the reply.

"What do you mean, she gets worse?" I asked.

"Sometimes she comes from the bedroom and she is bruised all over. She never goes out, and you know how popular she used to be. I have been frightened to be here, but someone must stay. Sometimes the house is icy cold and smells foul. Then things begin to fall from the plate racks or paintings from the wall." She crossed herself. "She threw the crucifix we brought from Italy into the garbage," the housekeeper went on. "The finest priests in New York have been here, but they make her worse, so uncle said they must not come again."

"What about the boy?" I asked.

"He is all right but she takes no notice of him; he is frightened, but I have always managed to tidy up the mess before he sees it. I take him to the Lycée every morning and pick him up, but now her uncle says I must never leave Rose-Marie, so one of his boys comes and takes the boy to school in his limousine." It seemed as if the efficiency of the Mafia could cope with a case of potential possession.

"Uncle says will you please stay here," said the housekeeper. I nodded, as it seemed the logical thing to do. "You can sleep in my room and I will sleep on the sofa."

"No need to do that," I replied. "I would rather sleep on the sofa myself."

She was too well-trained to argue.

That night I prepared to sleep on the big, gilded, well-upholstered sofa, thinking to myself that it was no hardship to do so.

I settled myself down comfortably and put out the lights. Very tired after the journey, I dozed off and resolved to plan something the next day. When in doubt about anything, I find there is a great refuge in sleep. But this was not going to be my night to rest.

I awoke with a feeling that I was aboard the Queen Elizabeth and that we were going through a storm. The wind howled through the room and the sofa was swaying like a canoe taking the rapids. Horrible ear-splitting noises rent the air, and a hundred doors seemed to be opening and then slamming shut.

I put on all the lights, and the floor seemed to heave under my feet. I tiptoed to the bedroom doors. The boy was asleep; the housekeeper was awake but stricken with horror, bedclothes tightly clutched in her white-knuckled hands. I went to the door of Rose-Marie's room, but before I could open it, it was thrown open from the other side. Rose-Marie stood there, gaunt and disheveled, nothing like the beautiful girl I remembered. I stood in front of her. She moved like a zombie, ignoring me. She went to the sofa, picked up the sheet, pillow and blanket, stuffed them at the back of the sofa, and then turned again to me. "Rose-Marie," I said very softly, "this is Sybil, your friend. Don't you remember me?"

She hesitated, then rushed at me. I sidestepped, half expecting another attack, but she went into her room, closing the door with a tremendous crash. I heard the sound of pottery breaking, but not in the bedroom. I discovered it was in the living room. A porcelain lamp base was smashed to small pieces, but the electric light was still on. I stood for several minutes, listened, then decided to peep into the bedroom. Rose-Marie was in bed. I walked in and looked at her and to my horror found her eyes wide open, one eye huge and badly bruised. She hardly seemed to be breathing. I did not want to disturb her, so went back to the housekeeper's bedroom, and told her that everything was all right and that she must go to sleep. She had her rosary in her hands now, but trained as she was, she said she would try to sleep.

"Help us," she pleaded. Well, I was prepared to do that but right then I needed a good sleep. I retrieved the bedding from the back of the sofa and settled down again, leaving all the lights on. I awoke early, disturbed by the sound of the housekeeper preparing food in the kitchen before getting the boy off to school. I went into Rose-Marie's room; it was icy cold, although the rest of the house was pleasantly warm. I put extra blankets on the bed and prepared to draw the shades and the drapes.

An angry, moaning, inhuman noise came from the bed. I gathered she did not want to see the light of day, so I quietly left the room without doing anything else.

Somehow I had to break through that terrible nothingness in her eyes and let her know I was there. Every hour I went into the room and sat by the bed, looking into her eyes, constantly saying the same sentences to her again and again, to tell her I was there. Not a single sign of recognition. In the afternoon the chauffeur came to the door, saying he had instructions to take me for a drive and at the same time he delivered a large basket of wine and delicatessen produce to the housekeeper. She murmured approval. "Uncle is good to us," she said. "These are specially for you, and every day you must take a drive."

So every afternoon for a week I was whisked away in a superb limousine and driven through Central Park. There was little or no conversation between the driver and myself. At four P.M. I was delivered back to the apartment. If the routine for looking after my own health was the same every day, so was the phenomenon that occurred every night. Every time I lay down to go to sleep, some disturbance happened. Good crystal was thrown around, and the temperature would vary from stifling to icy cold.

Rose-Marie continued to be silent, and I steadfastly spent hours at her bedside. After two weeks, I was relieved to see a change in her eyes. She recognized me and said my name, then faded out again, complete with gusty winds, smashed crockery, and the shaking of the floor and walls.

I was now quite reconciled to living in this strange world, determined to break through the silence of my dear little friend. I ate well, drank good Italian wine, but had little sleep and was very irate that the phone could not be used.

"It is tapped," said the housekeeper, "so it's better to make calls from a phone booth. Uncle says we must not use the phone. Of course it all happened after the dreadful business here."

I did not ask what the business was; I could guess. Uncle was in exile and therefore could not come to New

York to see his niece. I was a stand-in for a Mafia chieftain and suffering another kind of war.

Time was galloping along, and I knew I had to get through to Rose-Marie. Sometimes she was badly bruised on her body and face and the housekeeper tenderly cared for her, applying salves. She always emerged from the room with her eyes like organ stops.

On the eighteenth day the breakthrough was made. Rose-Marie talked to me. She thought she was recovering from a severe illness, and I did not disillusion her.

"I have nightmares," she said. "I dream that the whole apartment is full of evil and I am trapped in it."

I told her she was, indeed, trapped, but I explained that I could help. I did not disillusion her. I needed her cooperation though. I fixed a time, three days from then, when I was determined to exorcise the apartment and see what evil forces were really around. I explained this to her, and she seemed pleased.

"Whatever happens," I said, "I do not want you to leave your bedroom, so I am going to lock you in. I promise you will be safe, but on no account, no matter what you hear or feel, should you leave your bed. Try to think positively of happy days when we were in Italy."

On the twenty-first day I prepared to take action. I exorcised water by putting salt into it and dedicating it to the Mother Goddess. Helped by the housekeeper, I put salt and garlic in the corners of each room. The boy was sent to relatives in Brooklyn, since it was the weekend and he did not need to go to school. I tried to get the housekeeper to go, too, but she was adamant that she must stay in the place.

"All right," I said. "But only on one condition. You go

to bed. I will hypnotize you to sleep, and no matter what happens you stay there." She agreed.

At ten P.M. that night I hypnotized her and she fell into a good sleep. Rose-Marie was also asleep, but I did not entirely trust that, so I stood by her bed, all my concentration forced into willing her to remain asleep. I locked her in her room and put the key on the chain on which I wear the wonderful crystal I inherited from my grandmother.

Within an hour I had described a nine-foot-wide circle in the center of the room. I sat down in the center of it and was prepared to meditate there all night if necessary. I turned out all the lights but lit four candles and placed them within the circle, ceremoniously dedicating each candle to the four Watchers of the Night, starting from the east and working my way around to the north. I felt completely relaxed, the words of adjuration firmly in my mind.

The room resounded with clawing noises ranging from piteous catlike meows to deeper, wilder cries, as if the place had been turned into a zoo. Then came silence almost as unbearable as the noise. My hands, face and feet seemed as if they were encased in ice. I started on the incantations and the room seemed to reel. I was flung to the ground but got up as quickly as possible, giving but a fleeting thought that my kneecap was misplaced. No time to think of personal injuries; I knew worse must come.

In such an exorcism, fighting psychic forces, everything had to get worse before it could get better. A small picture fell from the wall, making far too much noise for so tiny an object. I hate to feel cold, and gradually I was freezing up!

247

"Think heat," I said to myself, remembering an old yoga exercise. "Think of the hot sun in California; think heat, heat, HEAT!"

It worked. The circulation came back to my legs and arms.

I have heard wolves baying in Canada, and it seemed I was surrounded by them. I kept within the circle, even when it seemed that snapping jaws were within inches of my face.

I continued the incantations, again and again, interrupted from time to time by out-of-this-world noises and occasionally an easy-to-recognize noise, such as several dozen people snoring and laughing at the same time. I told myself that only three people had any right to be in the house and anything other than these three human beings had to go.

"Depart, you evil spirits!" I yelled.

"Depart, depart, *depart!*"

My long hair seemed to be pulled from my head, but I continued. Then I heard what seemed to be the voice of the housekeeper calling for help from her room. On impulse I started toward her door and then realized that it was a trick to get me out of the sanctified circle.

"Depart, evil spirit," I called. "This is my domain, and I am stronger than you!"

There was silence for what seemed to be an eternity but in reality must have been only a few minutes.

Very clearly I heard a normal voice—Rose-Marie's—calling my name from her bedroom. Again I started to go toward her and remembered that I must not leave the circle. Grimly I yelled to the entities that they should depart. Thunder and lightning was the answer, and to my horror the drapes on the far side of the room burst

248

into flames! Again there was the temptation to rush from the circle and put out the fire, but I did not do so. The flames smoldered and the curtains died away.

Incantation. Adjuration. Incantation. Adjuration.

Keep awake, keep awake.

"Depart, evil spirits!

"I am stronger than you!

"Depart . . . depart . . . *depart!*"

The ceiling seemed to fall down, and the floor rose up to meet it. Still within the circle, I whirled on the floor, thinking the weight of the masonry must kill me, but it was an illusion. A final rushing wind blew everything from the marble mantel piece. I heard the shattering of glass and then silence. I sat within the circle for two more hours; then, as the dawn came up, I stepped out of it, tottering to the sofa. The room was a shambles. The big mirror over the console was cracked, flowers were scattered around, but I was alive and well. Best of all, the room seemed serene despite the disgusting mess.

I remembered the housekeeper and went in to bring her out of the hypnotic spell. She came out easily, rosary still gripped in her hand.

"It is over," I said, "but there is an awful mess to tidy up."

She bounded from the bed into the doorway to survey the scene.

"The devil had a party here last night," she said. I smiled at her.

"I guess he did." I left her bustling around in an effort to tidy up and went into Rose-Marie's bedroom. The key was still on the chain around my neck. But the door opened to my touch before I could use the key. I knew I had locked the door, but nothing now could surprise me.

Rose-Marie was just waking up.

"Draw the drapes, will you?" she said. "I just have to shower and then we can go out to lunch."

She still looked thin and ill, but there were no bruises and the strange vacant look had gone from her eyes. "I've been pretty sick, you know," she said. "But today I feel good and I am so happy you are here. We'll have fun. When do you have to return?"

I knew it was all right to leave, but I stayed on a few days. The hard-working housekeeper tidied up the debris. Rose-Marie remarked on the mirror and wondered what had happened, but expressed no dismay about the broken procelain.

"We can go on a shopping spree," she said. "I love spending money."

For the next few days we lived like millionaires, using real money as if it were going out of style. Uncle never liked credit cards. We visited every Italian relative in Brooklyn and had a ball. I was almost reluctant to return to California, but the time came when I got inside the sleek, black limousine and was whisked off to the airport. Los Angeles, which I always thought a mad city, was a haven of rest after the visit to New York. All the time I was there, flowers, fruits, imported wine and baskets of delicatessen goodies arrived at my house. Not a single package had a note on it, and my friends teased me about the constant flow of goodies. I could not tell them that Uncle was an appreciative gentleman and that the Mafia never forgets a good deed. It would have been as absurd as telling them that the presents were a bonus from the devil!

Hollywood, the city of a million fantasies, was not yet ready to appreciate a single fact. It was a long time before possession and exorcism became conversation pieces. Hollywood was too busy coping with its own spectacular version of the occult explosion: *Night Gallery* and Vincent Price specials.

The worst had yet to come.

And it did.

Bibliography

Alexander, W. M., *Demonic Possession in the New Testament* (Edinburgh, 1902).

Bernal, J., *The World, the Flesh and the Devil*, (London, Jonathon Cape, 1970).

Bibliothèque Diabolique, Vols. I, II and IV (Paris, 1822).

Brognolus, C., *Manuale Exorcistarum* (Italy, 1683).

Burstein, Sona R., "Demonology and Medicine in the 16–17th Century," *Folklore*. Volume LXVII, March, 1956.

Corus, Dr. P., *History of the Devil*, (London, Kegan Paul, 1900).

Galagala, J., *Memoir: Swiss Bibliotheque Universelle*, June, 1896.

Kerner, Justnus, *Die Geschichte de Madchens von Orlach*, reprint (Schwab Hall, 1898).

Mengus, H., *Compendio dell Arte Essorcistica et Possibilita Della Mirabili*, MDXC (Bologna, Italy).

Mengus, H., *Flagellum Daemonum: Exorcisms Terribles Pontissimi et Efficaces*, MDLXXXII (Italy).

Noydems, D., *Practica de Exorcistas* (Paris, 1666).

Religious Encyclopedia (London, Funk and Wagnall, 1909).

Sinclair, P., *Satan's Invisible Hand* (London, 1814).

Thompson, R. Campbell, *Devils and Evil Spirits in Babylonia*, 2 vols. (London, 1903–4).

Unger, M. F., *Biblical Demonology* (Scripture Press, n.d.).

Wahre Geschichte der Befreiung eines vom Teufel Besessenen, translated from *Review der Missioner*, 1882.